ZEN ECONOMICS:

SAVE THE WORLD AND YOURSELF BY SAVING

ROBERT VAN DE WEYER

BOOKS

Winchester, UK
Washington, USA

ZEN ECONOMICS:

SAVE THE WORLD AND YOURSELF BY SAVING

Copyright © 2004 O Books
46A West Street, Alresford, Hants SO24 9AU, U.K.
Tel: +44 (0) 1962 736880 Fax: +44 (0) 1962 736881
E-mail: office@johnhunt-publishing.com
www.johnhunt-publishing.com
www.0-books.net

U.S. office:
240 West 35th Street, Suite 500
New York, NY10001
E-mail: obooks@aol.com

Text: © 2004 Robert Van de Weyer
Design: Graham Whiteman Design

ISBN 1 903816 78 5

A CIP catalogue record for this book is available from the
British Library.

Printed in Singapore by Tien Wah Press (Pte) Ltd

CONTENTS

PROLOGUE

FIGURES OF TRAGEDY

In the opening years of the twenty-first century, as we survey the unfolding drama of human history, there are at least five figures that can bring tragedy – five reasons for being acutely anxious.

The first and most prominent tragic figure is militant religiosity. There are growing numbers of Muslims, Christians, Jews and Hindus who believe their own faith possesses some kind of spiritual monopoly, so that they regard the adherents of other faiths as spiritual enemies. And this conviction readily expresses itself in acts of violence. Militant religiosity is most manifest within Islam, in which, as the entire world cannot forget, the perpetrators are sometimes willing to sacrifice their own lives. But Israel's devastating response to Palestinian suicide bombers is undoubtedly fuelled, at least to some degree, by religious conviction; indeed many Israelis believe that the Jews have a divine mandate to occupy the lands where the Palestinians now live. The influence of Christian fundamentalism on American foreign policy is more indirect, but many Americans undoubtedly believe that their country's huge military superiority is in some respect divinely ordained, and therefore can be exerted with a sense of moral superiority. Violence perpetrated by Hindus in northern India is a grim reminder that even a religion imbued with the ethos of peace can in the present age turn extremely nasty.

The second tragic figure is the widening economic gap between the countries of the world. Incomes in north America and Europe have continued to double every thirty years or so, as they have done since the nineteenth century; and incomes in some east Asian countries have more than quintupled within the last thirty years. At the same time incomes in large parts of Africa have actually fallen, while in the Middle East and other parts of Asia they have stagnated. The increasing flow of migrants from poor countries to rich ones, defying border controls and running huge risks, is a symptom of widespread economic despair. And there are certainly links, albeit quite subtle, between economic inequality and religious militancy. Although some of the leading Islamic militants come from the wealthy elite of their countries, the poverty of much of the Muslim world breeds a sense of humiliation, and thence resentment towards the West; and the repeated condemnations by Muslim clerics of western decadence twist this resentment into righteous hatred. Conversely America's capacity to afford its vast military forces is readily taken as evidence of divine approval, within Protestant Christianity, which flourishes in America, spiritual salvation and economic success have long been bedfellows.

The third figure is global warming. Although a few experts still doubt whether it is actually occurring, the potential damage of a hotter global climate is so great that the case for acting against it is overwhelming. Even now there seem to be more floods and droughts than a few decades ago; and it is conceivable that in the new century natural disasters could cause as much death and misery as mass warfare did in the last century. Yet every international effort during recent years to reduce the emission of the relevant gases has foundered. Humanity as a whole seems to lack the impulse for self-preservation that individual human beings possess.

The fourth figure is the decay of public services. During the twentieth century governments across the world took upon themselves the provision of education, health care, and transport infrastructure and they raised tax rates accordingly. In America about a third of all income is taken in taxes, while in some European countries the government consumes almost half of the national cake. Yet amidst the private affluence of Europe and America, there remains great public squalor, in the form of overcrowded schools, long queues for medical treatment, and congested roads. And when governments try to overcome the public squalor by raising taxes, they threaten the economic dynamism on which tax revenues depend. In poorer countries the dilemma is somewhat different, but no less acute. Many of their governments, as they became independent from European empires, spent lavishly on public services, believing that this would stimulate economic growth, which in turn would boost tax revenues. But the growth failed to occur, and so the public services must be cut – a point that the International Monetary Fund frequently reiterates.

The fifth figure is demography. There is a remarkably strong connection, seemingly in every country and culture, between income and the birth rate: as people grow richer, they have fewer children. In poorer countries the birth rate remains extremely high, so that their populations rise far faster than their economies can grow. As a result living standards fall and unemployment rises. While the AIDS epidemic has only a small effect on population growth, it is causing great economic damage, since a high proportion of the victims are skilled young men, hence the birth rate will remain high. In many richer countries by contrast the number of births has fallen far below the rate necessary to replace the population, and also people are living far longer. As a result the proportion of elderly people is rising rapidly. This is beginning to put acute pressure on the provision of pensions. Many men and women now in their middle years face the prospect of spending their old age in poverty.

JESTER IN THE CORNER

In the far right hand corner of the global stage is a figure whose appearance and behavior is quite strange and peculiar. Through the twentieth century, and especially from the 1950s, Japan adopted and emulated western industrial methods, achieving astonishing rates of economic growth. By the early 1980s Japan seemed set to surpass even the United States. Then at the end of the 1980s, while the economies of north America and Europe continued to move forwards, entering their longest boom in history, Japan stalled – and has remained stalled ever since.

While many people in the West are aware of Japan's stagnation, most assume that the source lies in some particular problem of the Japanese economic system, or even some inscrutable aspect of the Japanese psyche – and thence dismiss Japan from their minds. And when experts point to the propensity of the Japanese banks to make bad loans, implying that this may be the cause of Japan's economic sickness, westerners feel secure in the conviction that their own banks are too flint-hearted to be so foolish. Yet western thinkers from the past – John Maynard Keynes and Karl Marx most notably – would have little difficulty in diagnosing the main cause of the Japanese dilemma: thrift. Japanese households now typically save almost a third of their disposable incomes, while western households typically save less than a tenth.

Marx and Keynes both recognized that at an early stage of capitalist development, when factories are being built and large amounts of heavy machinery are required, thrift is vital. Indeed the sociologist Max Weber believed that the Protestant emphasis on the virtue of thrift underpinned the original capitalist economies of northern Europe. And Japan's habit of thrift was crucial to its economic explosion in the middle years of the twentieth century. But as Keynes and Marx observed, there comes a point of capitalist maturity in which thrift becomes a social vice. Keynes referred to the paradox of thrift, by which the thrift of an individual makes that individual wealthy, whereas thrift practiced by everyone makes everyone poor.

The role of the jester is to appear absurd, and yet to convey wisdom. To most in the West Japan's thrift seems like an absurd affront to the values on which its own economic prowess has been built. Surely, westerners think, the only point of working hard and creating successful companies is to enjoy the fruits of those efforts. Yet Marx and Keynes were both inclined to think that in mature capitalist economies people would be inclined to produce far more than they felt inclined to consume, and to save the surplus. In the first part of this book we shall look at the phenomenon of thrift in modern affluent societies, especially in the light of those five tragic figures; and we shall see that thrift is indeed rational and shrewd. In fact, it appears so rational and shrewd that households in western countries are likely at some point to copy the Japanese example.

Japan is, of course, famous for its Zen sages who taught wisdom through absurdity. Thus we may call thrift in affluent societies Zen economics – or, more precisely, personal Zen economics, since it refers to the economic choices of individuals.

GLOBAL CLIMAX

Zen sages have taught that the forces of change gather strength quietly, and then suddenly erupt. Modern chaos theory has given mathematical credence to this notion. And history also affirms it. Obscure conflicts over land in central Asia, forcing populations to shift westwards, ultimately led to the collapse of the Roman empire. A religious movement amongst unsophisticated tribesmen in the Arabian peninsula led within a few decades to the collapse of two other empires, and the creation of a new Muslim empire stretching halfway across the world. Debates in draughty monastic cloisters and university halls led eventually to the acceptance within Europe of the scientific method, and thence to a surge of scientific and technological progress that continues to gather momentum. The development in the hills of northern England of a technique for organizing work, the division of labor, led with astonishing speed to the industrialization of Europe and north America – and ultimately to the appearance of Sony, Mitsubishi, Toyota and the other industrial giants in Japan. In the same way the thriftiness of the Japanese may prove to be the harbinger of change that will transform the world.

Marx and Keynes both believed that excessive savings in mature capitalist economies would lead to a crisis of capitalism, marked by declining income and rising unemployment. Marx looked forward to this crisis with glee, believing that it would trigger a workers' revolution and the inception of socialism. Keynes wanted to preserve capitalism, and advocated high government spending to make up the shortfall in private consumption, thus restoring full employment. But the Japanese experience suggests that Keynesian policies are now futile. The Japanese government has spent money lavishly, even at one stage giving households consumption vouchers; and they have also tried to give money away by reducing the interest rate to zero. Unfortunately the stubborn Japanese consumer has remained unimpressed, and the only consequence is that the Japanese government has incurred massive debts.

Yet visitors to Japan are not struck by the misery of the people, apart from the relatively small number who have lost their jobs – on the contrary, there seems to be quite a high degree of contentment. The reason is that they are responding rationally to the nature of modern, mature capitalism; and sooner or later the people of other mature capitalist societies will respond in much the same way. Nor does Japanese society appear to be on the brink of collapse – on the contrary it appears gradually to be adapting to the thriftiness of its people. And as and when Japanese thrift spreads across the globe to Europe and north America, the consequences will be largely benign for the world as a whole.

The part of this book entitled *Saving Economics* analyzes the likely reactions of mature capitalist economies to a much higher level of savings. It will conclude that higher savings do not necessarily lead to economic slumps, as Keynes and Marx suggested, there are forms of savings that can both maintain the economy at full capacity, and also have benign effects on human society as a whole. The following part, *Global Zen Economics*, will explore those forms of saving, and show how they may attack, wound, even ultimately destroy the tragic figures that haunt the global stage; at the climax of this drama, the jester will prove to be the hero.

AUDIENCE PARTICIPATION

If you become convinced that the drama described in this book is both plausible and desirable, then you will be eager to play a part in it. In particular, you will wish to become a practitioner of Zen economics, consuming less and saving more. The fourth part of this book, *Economical Saving*, consists of practical advice on how to do this. But this advice will be not be like that found in magazines and newspapers today: it will assume that other people are also trying to consume less and save more – that the drama has already begun. The best forms of investment are quite different when others are also trying to invest large sums.

There is a famous Zen *koan* about a man who falls off the edge of a cliff, and manages to clasp the branch of a shrub with his teeth, preventing himself from plunging to the rocks below. Another man comes along, and asks him if he wants any help. Like all Zen *koans* it has many meanings. But one of its meanings seems to be that, as soon as we see what we should do, we should do it. If this book convinces you of the wisdom of Zen economics, then you should enact it. As each additional person becomes a Zen economist, so it will be easier for the next person.

Sadly there are no known Zen *koans* about thrift. But the Zen sages apparently enjoyed puns. So we can imagine a present-day Zen sage saying: 'By saving you can save yourself and the world.'

PART 1: PERSONAL ZEN ECONOMICS

THE CIRCLE OF IRRATIONALITY

Two centuries ago, when Britain was beginning to industrialize, the atheist intellectual and social reformer Jeremy Bentham (*) asserted that our desire for goods and services diminishes as we consume more. This is manifestly true of any particular good: the second chocolate or burger gives less additional pleasure than the first, the third gives less than the second, and so on. Bentham also said the same about consumption as a whole: that as we consume more goods, the pleasure and satisfaction from consuming additional goods becomes less and less. He drew the interesting conclusion that the total happiness of society can be increased by redistributing income from the rich to the poor, since the additional pleasure for the poor of spending their extra income will be greater than the loss of pleasure to the rich. If Bentham had anticipated the continuous economic growth that Britain and other countries in Europe and north America have experienced since his time, he would have predicted that people would become more and more weary of consuming, and would thus save an increasing proportion of their income. And Keynes, in his depiction of mature capitalism, adopted Bentham's view

But this did not happen. On the contrary, far from losing their appetite for goods and services, people have remained as ravenous as ever. Half a century ago, in *The Affluent Society*, John Kenneth Galbraith, offered an explanation of this phenomenon: companies not only produce goods, but they also produce the desire for those goods – leaving the consumers no better off than if the goods had never existed. According to Galbraith, most of the goods and services produced and consumed today satisfy no innate need, and could not even have been imagined by most consumers before they had been invented. The companies nurture the desire for their products by means of advertising and other forms of promotion. And now this phenomenon is spreading across the world, with the creation of global brands – a phenomenon famously analyzed by Naomi Klein in *No Logo*. Thus there is a circle of irrationality at the heart of modern capitalism.

Paul Ormerod in *Butterfly Economics* suggested that the human urge for emulation greatly augments the power of advertising, giving us an even stronger compulsion to consume whatever companies are producing. The circularity of production and consumption can be readily observed in the popularity in recent decades of trainers. Human beings in most climates need to wear shoes on their feet, and a strong, comfortable pair of shoes could probably be manufactured and sold for about 20% of the typical price of trainers. At the outset of their global conquest Nike, Reebok and Adidas were hugely successful in associating their peculiar style of shoes with sporting fitness. But once a certain number of cool young people were wearing trainers, then other youngsters simply wanted to copy them, and advertisements merely reinforced this urge. And the trainer manufacturers have exploited this same symbiosis of advertising and emulation with each new variation on the style.

Ormerod compared human behavior with that of ants. He described an experiment in which two sources of food were placed at an equal distance from a nest of ants. One might expect the ants to choose randomly between the two sources, which were constantly replenished, so that the consumption from each would be roughly the same. But ants, when they have found a source of food, leave a chemical secretion that stimulates other ants to go there. Thus once the first ant leaving the nest had discovered one of the sources, the other ants followed. Also, whenever the chemical secretion was obliterated, perhaps by a rain shower, the next ant might go to the other source – and then all the other ants followed. The movement of the first ant is akin to consumers who have been influenced by an advertising campaign – subsequent consumers are like the ants that follow the first ant. And a rain shower on the ants is like the appearance of a new product, backed by a fresh campaign, which induces a sudden change in consumer tastes.

There is, however, one important difference between ants and ourselves. Ants play no role in the actual production of the food they consume, but depend on the vagaries of nature, so their behavior varies greatly from day to day and season to season. In the capitalist economy, by contrast, new products are produced and advertised by people who are also consumers. Thus the directors and senior executives of our great companies are themselves victims of the irrationality that they perpetrate: they sell needless goods in order to buy needless goods for themselves. We have created a circle of irrationality, in which we spin round and round for year upon year, decade upon decade.

Since Galbraith wrote *The Affluent Society* real incomes in the West (actual income after the effects of inflation have been stripped out) have roughly tripled. We might expect to be slightly happier than we were then, since some of this additional output meets genuine physical and mental needs. Medical treatment is much improved, dentistry is less painful, our homes are warmer and less damp, we are able to buy more nutritious and tastier foods, and many more of us enjoy a good education. Also, although the invisible forms of pollution causing global warming are worse, the highly visible and unpleasant forms emerging from the chimneys of factories and homes are much reduced. But surveys inquiring into people's states of mind suggest that actually we are slightly unhappier. The main reason is that we find minor discomforts and irritations harder to endure. This is a further consequence of the circle of irrationality: our great companies lead us to expect a solution for every problem, and a cure for every ill; so when intractable problems and ills appear, we feel disappointed and even cheated.

Karl Marx, writing at a much earlier stage in our economic evolution, offered an even gloomier diagnosis. In 1844 (in the *Economic and Philosophical Manuscripts*) he asserted that the capitalist industrial economy 'alienates' people both from one another and from their work. In a society dominated by noisy factories and vast office complexes, human relationships are mainly impersonal and their work is meaningless. To assuage their inner emptiness and misery, people devote themselves to the accumulation of material goods with which to fill their homes: they become 'commodity fetishists'. Thus in Marx's view, the circle of irrationality arose through the breakdown of traditional communities – and the circle can only be broken by the creation of new forms of community. In fact, during the past twenty-five years most of the big factories have disappeared from affluent countries of the West, and computers have taken over the dreariest administrative functions. Many people have quite interesting occupations, working closely with others. Yet the circle of irrationality remains continues to spin. This does not mean that Marx's diagnosis is wrong. Commodity fetishism, like any strong habit, is hard to break.

In fact, Galbraith, Ormerod, Marx and others writing in a similar vein have understated the strength of the circle. The fables and fairy stories read by children have always featured merchants and landlords who devote their lives to acquiring wealth, and who become more miserable as they grow richer. They have no need for advertisements to stimulate their greed; it arises unbidden from within their hearts. Human beings, it seems, have always been susceptible to the illusion that an abundance of material goods is the route to happiness. Advertising merely exploits this susceptibility, and alienation enhances it.

The most famous story illustrating this illusion is the early life of the Buddha. According to the biography written by Ashvaghosha, the Buddha was the son of a king in northern India. His mother died when he was young, and his father became highly protective: he kept his son in a luxurious apartment in the palace, not allowing him to see anything that might disturb his mind. As the Buddha reached adulthood, he provided him with a beautiful wife who bore him a son. Finally, curiosity drove him to make a series of journeys outside the palace. The king tried to ensure that he only saw happy people along his route. But on the first journey a withered old man appeared, so he learnt about the inevitability of ageing. On the second journey a man with a disease appeared, so he learnt about the inevitability of sickness. And on the third journey he saw a corpse on the roadside, so he learnt about the inevitability of death. The Buddha concluded that no amount of wealth and luxury could protect him from suffering – and he left the palace in search of a form of happiness that is independent of material conditions.

While acknowledging the Buddha's wisdom, we are liable to conclude that he was exceptional, and that most of us are too weak to overcome our commodity fetishism – even though, unlike the Buddha, we have known its folly since childhood. And certainly it is rare for people to follow the Buddha in abandoning all material comforts. But the history of the twentieth century suggests that even in the modern world modest self-restraint is quite possible. In western democracies voters have frequently elected governments that promise to raise taxes in order to finance additional public services, and now most households pay well over a third of their incomes in tax. Collective restraint on personal consumption is no doubt psychologically easier than individual constraint, but the elections were honest and fair.

A more telling example occurred during the Second World War. At the outset of the War the economist John Maynard Keynes (in *How to Pay for the War*) recognized that households in Britain would need to reduce their consumption in order to release resources for the production of armaments. He recommended a scheme of voluntary savings in which the government would urge people 'to pay for the war' by buying bonds. The scheme was hugely successful. Of course, the specter of Adolf Hitler provided a powerful incentive. More importantly, perhaps, each individual household found it easier to cut back on its spending because other households were doing the same. Indeed, the experiment with ants suggests that, if there were a sufficient initial stimulus, a new fashion for high savings could take hold with great speed.

ZERO-SUM CONSUMPTION GAMES

We naturally assume that, if people are spending more money, they are securing for themselves a proportionately higher standard of living. And this is undoubtedly true for many of the things we purchase: through greater expenditure we can acquire more television sets, computers, cappuccinos and haircuts. Yet, as Fred Hirsch showed in The Social Limits to Growth, there is a wide – and widening – range of goods that are desired not for their intrinsic benefits, but for the fact that other people do not have them. Thus, in spending money and effort trying to acquire them, we are merely competing in a contest to sort out winners from losers. He called such goods 'positional', in that they relate to an individual's position in society.

The most obvious examples are goods that are acquired to confer status on their possessor. Only one person can have the grandest house in a town, and only a small number of people can have houses at which others gawp with envy. Most grand houses are several times larger than is needed to provide every conceivable comfort, so most of the money spent on building and maintaining them adds nothing to their inhabitants' living standards. Similarly, people buy large and expensive cars partly to impress others with the fact that they can afford such cars. Those responsible for determining the prices of Mercedes and Roll-Royce cars have long been aware that reducing the price would actually make the cars less attractive to purchasers. So the prices are set at a level that only the mega-rich can afford and numerous accessories are added to the cars to match the price.

Humbler versions of this game are played in every neighborhood, except perhaps in the direst slums. Some people feel impelled to acquire the latest electronic gadget, regardless of any benefits it might confer, in order to show it off to their friends. Others buy new furniture and kitchen fittings long before the old furniture and fittings have worn out, in order to keep a step ahead of the others in the street. And the model of car standing in the drive is the clearest possible signal of its owner's social aspirations. This is not to deny that new gadgets, furnishings and cars provide pleasure, but a large chunk of the pleasure derives from being amongst a minority that possesses them.

Holiday destinations are positional goods of a more subtle and pernicious form. The idyllic holidays shown in movies are at some isolated beach or lake of which the glamorous tourists have sole use, or in a remote oriental city where they are the only foreigners – apart perhaps from a few equally glamorous tourists. A generation or two ago most of the coast and islands of the Mediterranean and Caribbean seas offered such exclusivity. But the combination of higher incomes and cheaper air fares now enable hundreds of millions to go there, and as a consequence holiday resorts have been created that are remarkably similar to the resorts close to home where the majority used to stay during vacations. In the meantime the wealthy elite must devote even more money to hunting down places that they alone can afford.

In most western households expenditure on housing, domestic goods, cars and holidays absorbs well over two-thirds of total disposable income. We can reasonably guess – and nothing more than a good guess is possible – that around half of that spending is positional. It follows that a third of our total spending is being wasted on an economic competition from which the population as a whole gains nothing.

But this significantly understates the reality. There is one major area of expenditure that we fondly believe to be entirely benign and beneficial, yet where the positional element is especially large – education. Public expenditure on education grew hugely in affluent countries in the latter half of the twentieth century, so it typically accounts for almost a fifth of total government spending. And private spending on education is now rising rapidly, with private schools enjoying record levels of demand, and many parents employing private tutors to give their offspring additional help at weekends and during vacations. Politicians are convinced that high levels of education are essential to achieving high rates of economic growth, and there is undoubtedly a correlation – although not as strong as many imagine – between a country's prosperity and the educational attainment of its population. It does not follow, however, that education causes prosperity. The correlation is equally consistent with the notion that as people grow richer, they buy, or vote for, more education – that prosperity causes education.

There is a connected, and much stronger correlation between an individual's prosperity and educational attainment. Educational economists calculate the rate of return of different educational qualifications. They add up the costs of attaining a qualification, including both the direct costs such as tuition, and also, in the case of higher qualifications, the loss of earnings while people study. Then they look at the average difference between the lifetime earnings of people with that qualification, and those without it – and they compute this difference as a percentage of the cost. Not surprisingly it turns out that investing in a Bachelor's and Master's degree has a very high rate of return – it is extremely profitable. Educational economists assume that higher earnings reflect greater productivity; and this is taken to explain why countries with a highly educated population tend to be prosperous.

The economist Kenneth Arrow has proposed a quite different explanation. He suggests that differences in natural ability are the main causes of differences in earnings. The educational system is a prolonged, and extremely expensive, aptitude test, distinguishing these differences. In particular, the longer that young people can remain within the system, and the higher the academic level at which they survive, the more intelligent they are proving themselves to be. Thus spending three years at Cambridge (Massachusetts or England) does not in itself make you more productive, but the fact that you gained a place at such a distinguished university, and successfully completed the course, indicates that you are a person of exceptional intellect, and therefore will perform well in very important – and thence highly paid – positions. Arrow does not deny the economic importance of basic educational skills such as reading and arithmetic, and he affirms that a few occupations, such as medicine, require a large body of knowledge that must be absorbed in advance. But the skills for most occupations must be acquired on the job itself and prior education merely indicates the likelihood of individuals being capable of acquiring those skills.

Arrow's theory is virtually impossible to test scientifically. Nonetheless, once stated, it seems to some degree self-evident. Those in past generations compelled to learn Latin and ancient Greek often wondered what use these dead languages would be in later life. The relevance of history, geography and literature in the modern school syllabus is equally obscure, and many of the subjects studied at university, such as philosophy and political theory, seem to make a virtue of irrelevance. Even fields of study such as business and management, which purport to be equipping young people with useful skills, contain large chunks of purely academic knowledge. It was often said that grappling with the syntactical complexities of Latin and Greek trained the young mind, so that in adulthood it could adapt itself to any occupation, and the same economic justification is offered for much of today's education. But it is far from clear that this mental training needs to last as long as two decades, which is the period most youngsters now spend in educational institutions.

There is, of course, another very potent reason for education: it is form of consumption that yields profound and lasting satisfaction. Indeed, for many people the acquisition of knowledge is one of their greatest pleasures. Unlike almost all other pleasures it increases, rather than diminishes, the more that it is enjoyed. Thus by nurturing in our children a love of learning, we immeasurably enrich their lives. But if we recognized this as the primary purpose of education, then we should spare our youngsters much of the educational misery that actually suppresses this love. No longer would we cram them to attain high grades and no longer would we compel them to study subjects for which they are manifestly unsuited or unready.

As western societies become more affluent, so an increasing proportion of our income is spent in the chase for status. Most households now have all the goods and services that can make a genuine contribution to their material and psychological well being, so additional expenditure is devoted largely to positional goods. And in the vivid phrase of games theorists, the chase for status is a zero-sum game: one person's increase in status is another person's decrease.

But as with any game, people are free to opt out of the status chase. The losers are likely to be the first to withdraw. But even the winners, as they realize how much money they are spending on it, may begin to question its value. And the more people that opt out, the fewer are the rewards for those who stay in: there is no satisfaction in having a swanky house and car if your neighbors and colleagues take no notice. Thus a rejection of the status chase, once it began, would tend to gather pace. One can even imagine a kind of inverted status chase becoming popular, in which status symbols become objects of derision. This inversion would conform to the teachings of all the great sages of the past, from Plato, Seneca and Christ, to Lao Tzu, the Buddha and the Zen masters. And, somewhat paradoxically, it would conform to the ethos of the great universities to which ambitious young people struggle to gain entry. University professors traditionally take pride in driving battered old cars, wearing worn-out jackets, and furnishing their crumbling homes with creaking tables and decaying chairs – thereby displaying their contempt for positional goods.

The Japanese seem to be opting out with particular ease, because their culture has for many centuries placed a high premium on conformity. Thus even at the height of their capitalist boom, they viewed chasing status with suspicion. Status chasing has a much longer pedigree in western cultures. The current cult of celebrity seems to suggest that being at the top of the status pile is more important than ever. But western cultures have an even longer tradition of civic pride, in which people take satisfaction from the achievements of their local community. During the capitalist resurgence of the 1980s and 90s civic pride seemed dull and old-fashioned, but as people realize how little their lives have improved through two decades of boom, the fashion is likely to change.

Even in Japan, however, educational cramming remains as popular as ever. While adults may be willing to withdraw from the status chase, they are reluctant to pull their children out. They naturally want their children to have the widest possible choice of adult occupation and high educational attainment is the means to this. There is no incentive for prospective employers to develop their own aptitude tests since the educational system performs this function quite adequately – and the government and the parents pay for it. But as voters people may wise up, and demand that their governments stop subsidizing courses that are neither useful nor enjoyable.

CONSUMPTION STRESS

The most expensive item consumed by most households is space. The purchase price of one square meter or yard of floor area in a typical town or city of western Europe and north America is around 1500 euros, or a similar amount of dollars; in very desirable areas it can be ten times that figure. The annual cost of renting one square meter or yard, which in effect is the annual cost of consuming that space, is about 5% of the purchase price – so 75 euros or dollars as an approximate average, rising to 750 dollars or euros in expensive property.

Yet in our use of space we barely consider this cost. When we are wondering whether to buy a particular item for our homes, we think only of the cost of the item itself, not the cost of the space it will absorb. And we continue to store things in our homes that we are unlikely ever to want. Most of us regularly use only a small proportion of the utensils that cram our kitchen cupboards; the other utensils symbolize our forlorn hope of cooking more adventurously. Our wardrobes bulge with garments and shoes that we purchased impulsively and have barely worn. Discarding them would be an admission of folly that we are reluctant to make. Against the walls of the typical living room are articles of furniture – chests, cabinets, chairs – that once served a good purpose, but now are neither practical nor decorative. When in later years people move into a smaller house or apartment, and are thus compelled drastically to reduce the volume of their possessions, they rarely miss what they throw out, and usually feel relieved.

For those owning their home profligacy in the use of space has in recent decades seemed quite lucrative, so there has been little incentive to economize. Property prices have usually risen faster than other prices, and also faster than salaries, so the floor area filled by unwanted goods has generally been an appreciating asset. But it has not been as a safe an investment as many imagine. There have been periods when property prices have dropped sharply. During the 1970s property prices throughout the western world rose far more slowly than inflation, so in reality they fell. Also there have been very large regional variations. While homes in the most salubrious neighborhoods of London, New York and Munich have multiplied many times over in value, there are towns in old industrial areas where houses have become almost worthless.

It seems possible – even likely – that the period of home-owning as an investment is coming to an end. The surge in property prices in the late 1990s was primarily caused by falls in short-term interest rates, which in turn reflected the slaying of the inflationary dragon. Lower interest rates enabled people to service larger loans. Existing homeowners reacted by trying to buy the larger homes, and younger people rushed to buy the smaller homes. Since the supply of housing cannot suddenly increase, the higher demand simply translated into higher prices. In the first years of the new century the central banks pushed interest rates down even further to avert an economic recession, and this added further fuel to the fire of housing demand. The most conspicuous symptom of the impending recession of 2002 was rapid falls in share prices and dividends, and so many people decided to buy additional property in order to rent it out – causing the flames of demand to rise even higher.

But none of this fuel can be used again. Interest rates cannot fall much further; and property rents as a proportion of prices will soon fall so low as to match the dividends on shares.

In Japan the fire stopped burning over a decade ago, and has been followed by a very cold shower. During the 1980s property prices in Tokyo rose to dizzying heights, so at one point it was claimed that the land occupied by the emperor's palace was worth more than the whole of California. The price of golf-club membership – golf being a very space-consuming activity – multiplied tenfold. But since the end of the 80s the price of housing in Tokyo has approximately halved, while the price of golf club membership has fallen back almost tenfold. Far from being a good investment, property in Japan has proved an extremely bad one – although not as bad as investing in the Tokyo stock market. As a result Japanese families have come to regard the floor space of their homes as a consumption good like any other, and they have become adept at economizing on its use.

This has undoubtedly been an important factor in inducing the Japanese to save more and consume less. Floor space is a rather special kind of consumption good, in that it complements a large number of other goods: in order to consume electronic gizmos, furniture, kitchen utensils, and so on, we need room. Thus, if people try to economize on floor space, they inevitably economize on those other items as well. The typical Japanese family has wisely decided that it has no need of more possessions. On the contrary, it will only buy something new if it is better or smaller than something it already owns – and hence can either improve the use of space, or yield additional space.

While space is expensive, time is scarce and growing scarcer. And time, like space, is both a complement to all other goods, and something that we habitually fail to take into account. When we buy something, we not only ignore its bulk, but we are also inclined to forget how long it will take to consume. A CD takes an hour or more for each hearing, and a DVD two or three hours for each viewing – hence CD and DVD players demand days, weeks and months of our attention. Taking memorable stills on a camera, or memorable movies on a camcorder, requires great patience. There is no point in having the latest cookery equipment if you habitually buy pre-cooked meals from the supermarket and pop them in the microwave. A bottle of fine French wine should be sipped slowly over the course of an entire evening. Indeed virtually every good and service is time-consuming to consume.

More than three decades ago Linders, in his book *The Harried Leisure Class*, observed the stress of consumption and noted the various strategies we adopt in order to cope. The simplest is to store the items that we do not have time to enjoy, assuring ourselves that one day we shall get round to using them. As a consequence, not only do our cupboards bulge with costly detritus, but so also do our attics and garages. Another common ploy is what he calls 'simultaneous consumption', in which we attempt to consume several goods at once. Thus we eat while we are watching television and we read a magazine and drink wine while we listen to a CD. And we rapidly replace the goods that we have, buying new clothes when the old ones are almost as good as new, and changing the curtains and carpets before even the slightest signs of wear are visible. Indeed, rapid changes in fashions, which are a prominent feature of modern societies, are arguably an expression of consumption stress: consumers eagerly collude with producers in making last year's tastes seem dull and vulgar, and thence impel themselves into making fresh purchases according to this year's tastes.

Our shortage of consumption time has considerably worsened since Linders' observations. Now women typically have full-time jobs, taking only a few weeks or months away from work if and when they give birth. Thus, like men, they too must cram their consumption into the evenings and weekends. The paradoxical result has been to increase, not reduce, the total amount of consumption. At times when the roads used to be almost empty, they are now filled with people rushing off to a theme park, a cinema or a shopping mall, as they strive to extract the maximum enjoyment from their scarce hours of leisure. And there are long queues at airports as hard-working couples board planes for weekend breaks. For many people consuming their income has become more intense and demanding than earning it.

Happily some forms of consumption save time, and thence ease consumption stress. In particular, efficient electrical appliances have eliminated much of the effort that our grandparents used to expend on domestic chores. Only forty or fifty years ago an entire day each week was devoted to washing and drying clothes – a task that now takes only a few minutes. At the end of every meal there was the lengthy ritual of washing and drying the dishes – a task now reduced to putting the dishes onto racks. And the availability of good pre-cooked meals can free people from the pots and pans – although they also deny people the therapy that cooking provides. One domestic chore, however, worsens as consumption increases: house cleaning. The widening gap between the incomes of the rich and the poor, another feature of modern economies, has enabled a growing number of high-income families to employ cleaners. But most of us continue to clean our own homes, and the time required to perform this chore multiplies according to the space we inhabit and the volume of goods we possess. Indeed, the effort of cleaning our possessions, and cleaning around them, is a weekly reminder of the folly of much of our consumption – a reminder that can only be avoided by living in squalor.

Since both space and time are so costly, the sensible response is to use them more carefully and sparingly. Time, like space, is a complement to many of the other things that we consume, so by reducing the amount of consumption, we reduce the pressure in space and time alike. When we allow ourselves to imagine the perfect domestic life, we do not envisage ourselves residing in a mansion filled with the contents of Harrods department store; a small cottage or a modest apartment, located in a quiet neighborhood and furnished with simple elegance, would be much more congenial. Nor do we see ourselves like visitors to Disneyland, rushing frantically from one amusement to another – we should prefer to relax amongst friends and to savor life's pleasures. Thus by economizing on space and time, and thence economizing on the rest of our consumption, we are likely to gain greater enjoyment. Almost two and a half millennia ago Epicurus, the Greek philosopher whose name has become synonymous with pleasure, observed that, over a certain level, consumption and pleasure are inversely related. Today few of us in the West can deny that we have reached that level, or far exceeded it; hence crude self-interest dictates that we save, rather then spend, any extra income we acquire.

FISCAL CRUNCH

There are a few goods, such as bread and bus travel, for which our demand falls as we grow richer. Economists call these inferior goods. At the other extreme there are superior goods for which our demand rises far faster than our incomes. Education, as we have seen, is undoubtedly a superior good. And even if people were less anxious about their children's final grades, they would still want their children to have good teachers in small classes. Health care is another superior good. We need to be physically fit in order to enjoy the fruits of affluence and we have become progressively less willing to tolerate any ailment that might interfere with our enjoyment. Moreover, as medical technology improves, so the best health care becomes steadily more expensive. Private transport, and the roads on which it runs, are also superior. It has been estimated that in western countries, for every 1% rise in personal incomes, people drive 3% more.

Education, health care and private transport are probably the three most important superior goods and, under our present arrangements, all of them are heavily dependent on governments. The arguments in favor of public provision are similar for education and health care. In the first place, both are said to bring benefits to society as a whole, as well as to the individual. A well-educated workforce, as we saw earlier, is supposed to raise the rate of economic growth, from which everyone benefits, and educated people are less likely to commit crimes. A healthy workforce may also improve economic growth, and universal health care reduces the risks to everyone from contagious diseases. Secondly, public provision operates as a collective insurance policy. People's need for health care is unpredictable and, when it arises, it is often very expensive. The need for children to be educated is predictable, but is concentrated. By paying for these things through taxation, we spread the cost over our lifetime. Thirdly, the rich pay more in taxes than the poor, so public provision slightly reduces economic inequality.

The first argument also applies to the building and maintenance of roads; good transport links are essential to economic growth. A second argument is that trunk roads between towns and cities are inevitably monopolies: it would be absurdly wasteful to have several roads, side by side, between Los Angeles and San Francisco, or London and Manchester. Thus if trunk roads were privately owned, with a toll charged to travelers – as was the case in many parts of pre-industrial Europe – the owners could exploit their monopoly power by setting the tolls absurdly high. Public provision prevents this. Thirdly, roads within town and cities are inevitably communal, in that everyone must have access to them, and communal goods must be communally provided.

But since education, health care and roads are superior goods, the costs of adequate provision to meet demand inevitably grows faster than our incomes, and to finance these costs tax rates must also rise. Yet, as the economist Laffer, famously observed, a point inevitably comes when higher tax rates actually reduce the revenues from taxation. In the extreme case, if tax rates were 100%, tax revenues would be zero, since the incentive to work would also be zero – so there would be no income to tax. At some rate less than 100% high taxes must suppress economic incentives sufficiently for tax revenues to begin falling – or at least to rise less fast than they would otherwise have done. Some economists have argued that tax rates in most western countries are already above this point. In particular, taxation is draining the funds that small business-owners have to plow back into their businesses, and since the growth of small businesses is the main engine of economic growth as a whole, high tax rates now are reducing the potential for tax revenues to rise in the future. Unfortunately, this is impossible to prove empirically. But the fact that

President Reagan's tax-cutting policies in the 1980s were followed by a surge in economic growth, and thence in tax revenues, is often taken as strong evidence. And the point remains that, even if we can never know the precise tax rate at which revenues start to fall, such a tax rate undoubtedly exists – and must be quite close to the present rates in western countries.

Laffer's logic has an extra twist when it is applied internationally. Taxes are levied by national governments, but decisions about large-scale investment are now to a great extent global. Thus by raising tax rates a government discourages transnational companies from establishing new branches in its territories, and encourages them to move existing branches elsewhere. This further suppresses the government's ability to raise tax revenue. Indeed, the international competition for investment not only prevents tax rates from rising, but also puts pressure on tax rates to fall. In principle governments could kill this competition by harmonizing their tax regimes, but even within the European Union this has proved politically impossible.

Long ago Galbraith coined the phrase 'private affluence and public squalor' to characterize the modern economy. He believed that higher taxation could bring public affluence. But if that time ever existed, it has now long passed: the demand for education, health care and roads already greatly exceeds the supply – and the gap between demand and supply can only widen. One consequence of this fiscal crunch is queuing: hospital patients may have to wait several months for appropriate treatment. Another consequence is overcrowding: many roads are almost permanently congested, and schools are overcrowded. A third consequence is decay: hospitals, schools and roads are not properly maintained or cleaned. Long car journeys offer a vivid illustration of the contrast between public squalor and private affluence: we pull off dirty roads where the traffic is crawling, and refresh ourselves in gleaming, spacious diners and restaurants.

Although no formal study has been made, there is evidence that grandparents are partly funding the rise in private education in some countries. Few parents can afford school fees out of current income, so grandparents subsidize the fees from their accumulated savings. As this practice spreads, so middle-aged adults, whose children have grown up, will deliberately increase their savings in preparation for the arrival of grandchildren. These same middle-aged adults have a further, and more selfish reason, to save more: to pay for private medical treatment in their old age. Thus we can expect that the fiscal crunch will greatly increase the proportion of income set aside by those in the latter half of their careers.

Although democracy is the father of many follies, it eventually tends to breed good sense. Sooner or later the proportion of people opting out of public education and health care will grow sufficiently large that governments will feel impelled to cooperate. They will start by offering tax breaks to people who pay privately for education and health care, so such people are not in effect paying twice over – through direct fees and through taxation. These tax breaks will encourage more people to save, and so overall savings will rise further. Then it will occur to governments that they should not be providing education or health care at all. Instead they should subsidize the poor, enabling the poor to join the rich in buying their own private health care and education. This will have the admirable effect of stimulating innovation. Governments, in their pursuit of popular approval, are inevitably reluctant to try new ideas, for fear of appearing foolish. But private providers of education or health care need only win the approval of tiny segment of the market, and if a new idea is successful, the potential rewards are great. The huge growth in recent decades in complementary therapies indicates how adventurous people are, even when their own bodies and minds are at stake. When the dead hand of government is lifted, this spirit of adventure will spread to the whole of health care and education.

It is more difficult to opt out of the use of roads. For some journeys we can use a train or an airplane, although usually we need a car to reach the station or airport. On routes where the volume of traffic is especially heavy, there could be competition between two or more roads, so the government could hand over the task of providing roads to private companies, allowing them to charge tolls. And the government could increase its own revenue by charging directly for all roads. Indeed, if some kind of electronic device were installed that could charge a higher price for a road at peak times, this would encourage us to stagger our journeys, thereby reducing congestion. But the simplest solution is for individuals to travel less. People may choose to live closer to where they work and amuse themselves. And in coming years, as digital communications become more ubiquitous and sophisticated, so more and more people will be able to do much of their work at home.

The city has been one of the greatest inventions of human civilization; indeed Aristotle regarded the city as the essence of civilization. By living side by side in close proximity, and on top of one another, we can come together easily for work and pleasure – and have little need for cars and roads. Cities in Aristotle's time were often no bigger in population than a large modern village, and since many modern businesses are quite small, there is no reason why some people cannot enjoy the advantages of living and working in quite modest communities.

And there is strong evidence that people are already reverting to Aristotle's view: house and apartment prices are rising fastest in neighborhoods close to where businesses, shops and recreational facilities are located. This in turn strengthens the pressure to economize on space, since space in such neighborhoods is by nature fixed in supply.

Cars, in addition to causing congestion, are extremely expensive to run. The annual cost of running a family saloon, taking into account depreciation and the cost of capital as well as the direct expenses, is about one fifth of average household income. So if congestion persuades us to become less dependent on our cars, we shall have more money to set aside for educating our grandchildren and treating our ageing bodies.

THE PENSION GAP

Half a century ago the life expectancy for men in western countries was just below seventy; and most young men left school and took a job at the age of around the age of fifteen. So the typical man worked for fifty years until the age of sixty-five, and then had four or five years of retirement. His widow was typically one or two years younger, and lived one or two years longer. There were numerous exceptions, of course: many of us have a great-grandparent that lived to the age of eighty or ninety, and perhaps another great-grandparent that died at forty of fifty. But in determining people's pension contributions the average length of life is what matters. And in those days, when the years of retirement were on average a mere one twentieth of the years of work, only a small fraction of a man's wage was needed to accumulate an adequate pension.

Today we can expect to live a whole decade longer; and we start work on average five years later. Also many people wish to retire earlier than the age of sixty-five, and many employers compel or persuade people to retire early, either as a means of reducing their workforce, or to hasten the promotion of younger people. So now the typical working life is around forty years, and the years of retirement around twenty years, the ratio has leapt from a twentieth to a half. Thus to accumulate an adequate pension people must set aside a far higher proportion of their monthly income.

This transformation in the ratio of work to retirement, and its effect on pension contributions, was disguised through the 1980s and 90s by rapid rises in the price of stocks and shares. Since pension contributions are mainly invested in the stock market, small amounts contributed through the 60s and 70s multiplied in value. The rise in the stock market was partly stimulated by inflation, which has a double effect: it increases the money value of the capital assets owned by companies and it raises profit margins, since costs are incurred at a lower price level than revenue is earned. Paradoxically the fall in inflation in the late 1990s, which led to a fall in interest rates, was a further stimulus: lower interest rates reduced the value of holding money in interest-bearing deposits, and so made shares more attractive – so the price of shares as a proportion of their earnings rose steeply. Even the fall in share prices from March 2000, following the pricking of the dot-com bubble, left the price/earnings ratio of many shares at historically high levels.

Although there will undoubtedly be bull markets in the future when share prices rise rapidly, we have moved to an era when the underlying trend will be only gently upwards. There are several reasons why inflation is unlikely to rise much above its present modest level in the foreseeable future, and interest rates are already as low as they were forty years or more ago. Thus the inadequacy of our pension contributions is now laid bare. Many of those who have contributed over a long period to a pension fund run by their employer, and who are now approaching retirement, are protected: the fund may be obliged to pay them a fixed proportion of their final salary. But others, whose fund promises to pay them a capital sum on retirement, will find that this sum is too small: the incomes from annuities, in which an individual pays a capital sum in return for a pension, have fallen drastically. Most people under forty will face poverty if they retire at sixty on the basis of their current level of pension contributions.

One way out of this dilemma is for governments to make up the shortfall. Indeed, some governments in western Europe, such as those of Sweden and Germany, already give quite generous pensions. But state pensions are funded out of current taxation, and so compete with other demands on the budget – for education, health care, roads, and so on. As we have seen, raising taxes even higher is likely in the long run to reduce tax revenues. Indeed, many in Germany and Sweden believe that the state's pension liabilities are already too high, and are wondering whether to reduce, not raise, state pensions in the future. So unless governments reduce spending elsewhere, they cannot raise pensions for the elderly.

Another way out of the dilemma is for people to retire later. For men and women to remain in gainful employment until their early or mid seventies would bridge the pension gap with ease. And in some areas of labor shortages some employers, such as large stores, are actively recruiting older people. But there are two obvious snags. The first is that many people are weary of the routine of work by their early sixties, and look forward to being able to pursue their personal interests while they still have energy and vitality. The second is that most people's abilities and skills begin to diminish even in their fifties; and they reach a point where the wisdom of experience no longer compensates. So those in professional and managerial positions, and those in jobs that required physical strength or mental agility, would face the prospect of demotion, or taking up a less demanding occupation. It seems unlikely that lawyers and computer analysts will happily become secretaries to their former subordinates, or will serve them lunch in the nearby pizzeria. A more realistic prospect is that many will try to augment their pension with some part-time work; indeed the older people already being recruited generally work fewer hours than their younger colleagues.

The third way of the dilemma is for people to save more during their years of work, and thereby augment the capital sum that they will have on retirement. Indeed, as people comprehend the size of the pension gap, and as stories circulate of people retiring from good careers and plunging into poverty, the rate of saving for old age will inevitably rise. Since much of these additional savings will be invested in company shares, share prices may rise and people may misinterpret this as the gap narrowing. But this rise would be fool's paradise, since it would not reflect a rise in the dividends being paid by companies, it would merely reduce still further the returns on shares – or, to put it the other way, it would increase still further the price/earnings ratio. Worse still, as this ratio rises, so the contribution of dividends to pension funds falls, and the cost of eventual annuities increases. Indeed, we may reach the situation when paying money into a pension fund is little different from stuffing it into a mattress: you can only take out what you put in. Thus if people wish in retirement to retain the living standards they enjoy during their years of work, they will need to put into the pension fund or mattress about a third of their income.

PART 2: SAVING ECONOMICS

WHAT AND WHEN

Meteorologists are now able to offer very accurate forecasts of the order in which different types of weather will occur: that, say, showers accompanied by a west wind will be followed sunshine with an east wind, and then it will become very hot and calm. They are less accurate in estimating the length of time that each type of weather will persist, so their daily forecasts can often be quite wrong. The reason for this discrepancy is that they have gained a profound understanding of the fundamental forces determining the earth's weather, but it is far harder to calculate the relative strength of each force at any particular moment.

Economists are similar when they peer into the future. They are quite accurate in predicting that particular economic events will occur, but less accurate in predicting precisely when they will occur. Their predictions are invariably based on the assumption that human beings are rational, and hence will make rational decisions. Although individuals often act irrationally, irrational actions in one direction by some individuals are usually cancelled out by irrational actions by others in the opposite direction. However, circumstances are constantly changing, so rational behavior also changes, and is difficult to know exactly when people will perceive and act upon any change.

We have analyzed five reasons why people in all affluent countries may adopt the thrift practiced by the Japanese. And they fall into two categories. The first three are reasons why consumerism – the persistent pressure to consume more and more – is adding less and less to people's happiness, and may even be subtracting from it. The last two are reasons for cut back on present spending in order to be able to spend more in the future. If these reasons are rational, as the analysis suggests, then we can be confident that at some point people will indeed become thriftier.

We can also predict the order in which these forces will impinge on people's minds. The pensions gap, which has been growing for many years, has been suddenly revealed by the decline in stock and share prices. It will take a little time for people to grasp its full implications, and a little more for people to decide how best to make extra provision for their retirement. Since most of the pension fund managers, as well as the army of financial experts on whose insights they depend, confidently predicted that the pension gap would be permanently bridged by rising share prices, their prestige has been severely battered. So when they invite people to put additional savings in their hands, the response may be coldly negative. Nonetheless trustworthy vehicles for people's money will eventually emerge.

These same vehicles will also carry people's savings for education and health care. Older people often complain that nowadays there is little difference between the policies of rightwing and leftwing political parties. They imagine that the dullness of politicians is to blame. But leftwing leaders know that raising taxes will not in the long run increase tax revenues, and rightwing leaders fear that people have become dependent on public services financed by taxation. Younger people by contrast seem to accept political paralysis as a fact of modern life and so larger numbers see no point in voting in political elections. This youthful realism is beginning to spread up the generations, expressing itself in a growing willingness to augment public provision with private effort.

But we cannot predict with any accuracy how soon all this will occur. While we perceive that the forces impelling people towards higher savings are strengthening, and those impelling them towards higher consumption are weakening, we cannot gauge precisely their respective powers. Thus we cannot forecast the moment at which the former will exceed the latter.

There is unfortunately a further respect in which economists are ignorant – and in which meteorologists are knowledgeable. Meteorologists can usually forecast the speed with which the weather will change; economists can rarely forecast accurately the speed with which human behavior will change. Sometimes behavior changes gradually, reflecting the gradual change of circumstances. But since human beings influence each other, changes in behavior, once they start, can gather momentum very rapidly. When the forces impelling higher saving exceed those impelling higher consumption, there may be slow increase in the proportion of income saved. Since actual reductions in consumption are uncomfortable, most households may simply devote the bulk of any additional income to savings – in this case it would take roughly a decade at normal rates of economic growth to reach Japanese levels of thrift. There may, on the other hand, be a quite sudden rise in average savings – as occurred in the 1970s in reaction to high inflation. A modest degree of austerity may become quite fashionable: more adventurous households may discover the art of austerity, and their lifestyle may be depicted in magazines and television programs, inducing others to copy them. Both scenarios are possible, but we have no way of knowing which will occur.

CRUSOE TO KEYNES

People landing on desert islands, such as Robinson Crusoe, face the most basic economic choice. They can either use their bare hands to catch fish and wild fowl for food, or they can set about creating nets and spears. If they use their bare hands, they will have something to eat immediately, but if they spend time weaving nets and carving spears, they will go hungry for a few days, and then have much more to eat. This is the choice, in its most primitive form, between consumption and savings: Crusoe has a single resource, his time; and he must decide how much of it to devote to obtaining goods for direct consumption, and how much to invest in making tools that will yield more goods in the future. And the choice for the great majority of people remained in this form until the eighteenth century: farmers and craftsmen alike had to decide how much of their time or income to set aside in order to obtain better tools for their work.

Industrialization transformed the way in which this choice is made. In a pre-industrial economy the decision to save, in the sense of setting time or money aside, and the decision to invest, in the sense of making or buying a new tool, is made by the same person. But in an industrial economy the decisions are divided: households decide how much of their income to save, and firms decide how much money to invest on new machinery, factory buildings, and so on. And there are various financial institutions, such as banks and stock markets, which channel funds from savers to investors.

Karl Marx was the first writer to recognize the huge importance of this division between saving and investment, and Keynes (in The General Theory) was the first to offer a coherent analysis of how its potentially disastrous consequences. Whereas in the pre-industrial economy savings and investments must always be equal in value, in the industrial economy the amount households plan to save is likely to be quite different from the amount firms plan to invest. And Keynes thought that in mature capitalist economies there was a tendency for planned savings to exceed planned investment: households have ample goods already, so it is easy for them to save, and this slackness of demand reduces the opportunities for profitable investment by firms. As a result mature economies, according to Keynes, have an innate tendency towards slump: lack of demand for both consumption goods and for machinery causes firms to lay off workers, and the unemployed workers have even less to spend, so even more workers are laid off. And as the economy slumps, so people can no longer afford to save as much as they had planned – causing the actual amount of savings to fall to the amount that firms want to invest. Hence at the heart of mature capitalism is a paradox: households save in order to become richer, but when the population as a whole tries to increase its savings, everyone become poorer.

Keynes formulated his theory of slumps in the period between the two world wars, when the western economies were in the midst of the deepest slump they had ever known, with unemployment in many countries at more than a quarter of the workforce. And he believed that the only solution was for governments to make up the shortfall in demand. To emphasize his point, he even proposed that the government pay unemployed people to put money in bottles and bury the bottles in the ground – and then allow the workers to dig up the bottles and spend the money.

Despite the evidence of their own eyes, many economists opposed Keynes, believing that a slump could only be a temporary phenomenon. They clung to a theory of capitalist equilibrium that dated back to David Ricardo in the early nineteenth century. Ricardo believed that, if the economy slumps and unemployment arises, workers will be forced to compete for jobs, causing wages to fall. Since wages comprise the main cost of production, prices will also fall. Lower prices will enable firms to export more goods abroad, and also people at home will find that their money is worth more, so they will spend more. This process will continue until everyone has a job, and the economy is functioning at full capacity. Keynes argued that Ricardo's theory was no longer applicable, since wages no longer fell in the face of unemployment: trade unions were strong enough to resist wage cuts and many jobs had long-term contracts that prevented these.

Hitler and Roosevelt settled the dispute in Keynes's favor. When Hitler and his National Socialists gained power in Germany in 1933, they embarked on a program of public spending beyond Keynes's dreams. Their expenditure on armaments was the economic equivalent of burying money and digging it up again. While loathing Hitler's political values, Keynes and his disciples pointed to Hitler's success in reviving the German economy. Franklin D Roosevelt became president of the US in the same year, and enacted the New Deal, a more modest program of public spending, and it too proved successful.

In recent years, however, Ricardo's theory has enjoyed a revival. Trade unions in most western countries are far weaker than they were in the middle of the twentieth century, and more and more work is undertaken on short-term contracts. Thus, the new Ricardians argue, if an economy begins to slump, firms will find it quite easy to reduce the wages, salaries and fees that they pay. This will cause prices to fall, and since people will find that their money is worth more, they will spend more. Needless to say, a new generation of Keynesians has also arisen, arguing that, while labor markets have become more flexible than in the past, wages remain quite sticky. Besides, even if wages, and thence prices, were to fall, there is no reason why people would spend more – instead they might decide to save the extra value of their money.

Japan seems to provide a new test-bed. Its experience since 1989 seems to give some support to both Keynesian and Ricardian theories, in that unemployment has risen and prices have fallen. But the rise in unemployment has been far less than Keynes would have predicted, and the level remains substantially lower than that in several European countries, such as Germany. And the fall in prices and wages has been far less than Ricardo would have predicted, suggesting that wages remain quite sticky. A third factor may also be operating: firms may be hoarding labor, and workers may be willing to accept a stagnant wage in return for greater job security. This phenomenon occurred in the old Soviet Union, and was known by economists as 'undertime' because it involves people wasting time at work. The redeeming virtue of undertime is that it prevents some people being thrown out of work altogether. But it cannot be sustained in a capitalist economy, since firms hoarding labor will simply not recruit new workers when old workers retire, so it merely delays the rise in unemployment. Thus ultimately Japan, like Hitler and Roosevelt, seems likely to vindicate Keynes.

WHY AND HOW

Keynes gave little consideration to the reasons why households save; he merely took as self-evident Bentham's assertion that, as people grow richer, the appetite for additional goods diminishes, and hence they set aside a growing proportion of their income. Yet while Bentham showed why saving becomes easier as incomes rise, he did not explain why people actually want to save. There must be some further reason as to why people wish to forgo present consumption in order to accumulate wealth.

Industrialization not only divided the act of saving from the act of investment, it also greatly weakened the economic bond between one generation and the next. In pre-industrial economies adults in their middle years provide for their elderly parents; indeed, typically all the living generations of a family live in the same house or compound. When the great industrial cities formed in Britain, and then elsewhere in Europe and north America, young men and women in rural areas, attracted by the wages paid in the new factories, abandoned their parents and went to live in tiny houses packed close together, each with only enough space for a nuclear family. And when the first generation of urban children grew to maturity and married, they went to live in quite separate houses. This same process is being repeated today in the new industrial cities of Asia, Africa and south America.

The consequence has been that elderly people in industrial societies must, largely or wholly, provide for themselves. Hence during their years of gainful employment they must accumulate sufficient wealth to meet their material needs during their final years. The economist Modigliani formulated this into a simple theory of savings: people save part of their earnings, and then spend their savings after they retire. This suggests that savings do not constitute a permanent loss of demand in the economy; rather, through savings people delay their demand. Indeed, if the population and the economy were stable, net savings in the economy as a whole would be zero. According to Modigliani's theory, therefore, there are four situations in which net savings will be positive. The first is where the population is rising, so there are more young people saving than there are old people spending their savings. The second is where young people want to have a higher living standard during retirement than their parents have, and so save more than their parents did. The third is where life expectancy is rising, so people must increase their savings in order to provide for a longer retirement. The fourth is where the returns of savings, such as dividends and interest, are falling, so people must save at a higher rate in order to accumulate a particular level of wealth on retirement.

As we have seen, the third and the fourth of these conditions now apply. The Japanese have seemingly awakened to this, and hence are saving avidly. It is only a question of time before people in the West also wake up, and decide to save more. But neither Modigliani nor Keynes gave much consideration to how people save. And whether higher saving will lead to a permanent slump, in accordance with Keynes's theory, or whether it will have a happier outcome, depends entirely on the forms of saving that people choose. There are three forms of saving that would not lead to a slump and each of these would potentially be very positive for human society, helping to resolve the profound problems that humanity now faces.

First, if savings induced a corresponding amount of investment, overall demand would remain unchanged. Keynes is undoubtedly right that within mature capitalist economies there are insufficient opportunities for investment. So the main effect of higher savings would simply be to increase demand for existing shares, bonds and property. This in turn would increase the price of shares and bonds without increasing their dividends and interest payments, and increase the price of property without increasing rents – so returns would fall, inducing people to save even more. The Japanese have tried to maintain returns on their savings by buying shares, bonds and property abroad, especially America, with the perverse result that Japanese share and property prices have slumped. But if savings had risen in America and Europe also, this escape would be impossible. By contrast, in most poorer countries there is a large savings gap: there are many potential opportunities for investment, but not enough savings to finance them. So if western savings were successfully channeled to these countries, their economies would grow, and as their economies grew, they would import more from the West, both consumer goods and machinery.

Secondly, if people saved by buying durable goods of high quality, there would be a change in the nature of demand, rather than a reduction in demand. In the past wealthier families typically purchased furniture of such high quality that it lasted several generations so an article of furniture was simultaneously a form of consumption and a form of saving. When electrical goods, such as washing machines and vacuum cleaners, first came onto the market in the mid twentieth century, many of them were so durable that they could last two, three or four decades. They were ultimately discarded because they became technologically obsolete, not because they wore out. Combining consumption with saving is an extremely efficient form of saving. And if westerners deliberately began to demand goods of high durability, they would also be reducing the amount of goods they consumed; they would be substituting quality for quantity. Thus the pressure on the natural environment would fall.

Thirdly, if people found ways of working and saving outside the capitalist system and worked fewer hours within the system, then lower demand in the economy would be matched by lower supply, so a slump would be avoided. In relation to capitalism, the effect would be the same as labor hoarding in Japan and the Soviet Union. But in relation to people's overall well being, the effect could be quite different. Time spent in religious activities that maintain and improve the state of the mind and the body, such as yoga and t'ai chi, may be regarded as a form of saving: effort is expended in the present for benefits that will accrue far into the future. And if far larger numbers engaged in these kind of activities, then religious attitudes in general might change. Open-minded forms of religion would grow in confidence, and so offer an alternative to religious fanaticism. Equally, if there were ways in which people could give time to the care of the elderly, in return for receiving care when they fall sick or grow old, this too would constitute saving. And this would help to overcome the perennial and worsening crisis that health care services are facing.

In the next part of the book we shall explore in more detail how these forms of savings satisfy the impulses to save outlined in the first part of this book, and also how they operate to overcome the global dangers described in the prologue.

PART 3: GLOBAL ZEN ECONOMICS

INVESTING IN THE SELF

Christianity was the first religion in history with global ambition: Christians came to regard conversion and adherence to their religion as the only means to personal salvation and well being; and therefore their explicit ambition was to convert the entire population of the world. This ambition was bound up with the way in which it defined itself: by the fourth century Christianity was understood as embracing a particular set of theological beliefs. The most important of these beliefs was that Jesus Christ, as described in the Bible, was the sole incarnation of God, and that only through his death God forgives people's sins. Manifestly the Christian creed is either universally right or entirely wrong, and Christianity set about trying to convince people of all continents and cultures of its rightness.

The second religion with global ambition was Islam, which came into being in the seventh century. It too defined itself in terms of beliefs: that there is a single God, who is supremely powerful, and that Muhammad is his messenger. Whereas Christianity in its fourth-century formulation implies that all other religions are wrong, Islam acknowledged Christianity and Judaism as partially true, in that Jesus and Moses had also been divine messengers, but the message delivered by Muhammad in the form of the Quran was full and complete.

Both Christianity and Islam proved adept at using political institutions as vehicles of growth. The Christian church organized itself on the same lines as the Roman imperial system, it established itself in every Roman colony, and eventually it persuaded the emperor himself to be its patron. Islam almost immediately created an empire of its own, that spread from north Africa and Spain in the west to Afghanistan in the east, and later Muslim empires carried Islam into India and beyond. Then from the sixteenth century onwards the great trading empires created by the European powers – Spain, Portugal, Holland, Britain, France and the rest – became conduits for a new kind of Christian evangelism which frequently identified itself with western economic prowess.

Confronted by the zeal of Muslim and Christian missionaries, other religions felt impelled to redefine themselves in term of beliefs. This was most explicit in the spiritual traditions of India. Although these traditions are very diverse, westerners in the early nineteenth century coined the generic term 'Hinduism' to delineate them, as if they constituted a single religion like Christianity and Islam, and Indians readily adopted this notion. Indian thinkers began to describe their ancient spiritual writings as 'scriptures', which, like the Bible and the Quran, should have authority over people's minds. And numerous essays and books were published which attempted to formulate a Hindu theology. Since the religious traditions of India are famously open and inclusive, most of these formulations applauded Christ and Muhammad for proclaiming the unity of God, but asserted that Hinduism pioneered this idea.

Yet theological belief is only one aspect of religion, and in some religions it plays no part at all. In Judaism moral and ritual practices have been central. So although most Jews hold strong theological convictions, people raised in the Jewish tradition, but who reject theology, can quite validly describe themselves as non-believing Jews. Indeed, at least two of the prime ministers of Israel have been non-believers. In Buddhism and Jainism self-transformation is the key. This is most clearly stated in the four noble truths of the Buddha: that there is no life without suffering; that the cause of suffering is desire; that suffering is eliminated by eliminating desire; and that desire can be eliminated. The way of eliminating desire is the eightfold path: right vision, right purpose, right speech, right action, right livelihood, right effort, right awareness, and right concentration. Jainism expressly denies the existence of a supernatural divinity, and teaches that all living beings may become divine by overcoming bodily attachments.

When Buddhism spread to China, and thence to Japan, various new sects were formed which promulgated particular theological beliefs. The most popular was the Pure Land sect: it taught that an enlightened monk called Amida had created a pure land of bliss, and that people could go there after death by constantly repeating his name. But the most powerful form of Buddhism in eastern Asia was Ch'an, as it was called in China – or Zen, as it became known in Japan; and the teachings of Zen are virtually devoid of any kind of theology. The essence of Zen is a form of mental training aimed at inner enlightenment, in which the individual enjoys profound and permanent serenity.

Seen in this way religion is an alternative economics. In our normal economic activities we seek to use our material environment in order to make and consume goods that satisfy our wants and desires. In our religious economics we seek to adapt ourselves, amending and reducing our wants and desires, so that we attain a higher level of well being at a lower level of consumption. Thus the time spent in the kind of mental training advocated by Zen is a form of investment, analogous to putting money into stocks and shares: we forgo some immediate pleasure in order to enjoy greater happiness in the future. Material economics and religious economics are not, of course, mutually exclusive – even the most enlightened Zen master needs food and shelter. But Zen and similar kinds of religion imply that the art of human happiness consists in finding the right balance – in finding the rational way of allocating our time and effort – between the two.

It is significant that the most inspiring spiritual leaders in history have come mainly from privileged families. Even Joseph, who raised Jesus, may have been quite wealthy: the Greek work describing his profession, which has usually been translated as 'carpenter', in fact means 'master-builder' or even 'architect'. And Francis of Assisi, the most popular Christian in history, was the son of a wealthy merchant. Muhammad belonged to one of the leading clans of the most prosperous tribe of Arabia, and the great Sufi masters of Persia were the sons of leading scholars and politicians. Within Zen itself the greatest master, Dogun, was the son of a government minister, while Shosan, another great master, belonged to the samurai, the warrior aristocracy. While the children of the poor may imagine that riches would bring happiness, the children of the rich understand from experience the truth of Jeremy Bentham's iron law of consumption – that additional pleasure diminishes as additional goods are consumed – and are thus prone to seek other means to happiness.

In the countries of Europe over the past two centuries, as people's incomes have grown and scientific knowledge has increased, there has been a massive rejection of theological religion. In north America the rejection has been less widespread. Nonetheless in both continents in recent decades there has been a growing interest in religions of self-transformation. The generation now approaching middle age is the first generation in history where the majority is both affluent, and grew up in affluent homes. Thus like Dogun and Shosan they have known the iron law of consumption from childhood. The visible expression of this religious awakening is the large number of people that enroll on courses and buy books teaching various kinds of self-transformation. Since these courses and books cost money, they make a modest contribution to overall consumption. But courses and books are useless unless their lessons are practiced in the privacy of the home, so the main expenditure is time. And as more and more people devote more and more time to self-transformation, so they may decide to work fewer hours for money. As a result this particular kind of saving – investing in the self – will suppress both demand and supply in the material economy.

The religion of self-transformation is already exerting a strong influence on Christianity – just as Christianity and Islam once influenced other religions such as Hinduism. Christians today frequently put great emphasis on 'spirituality', by which they mean meditation and other disciplines cultivating inner tranquility and calm. The term was virtually unknown a few decades ago, and the great Christian preachers of past generations would mostly have poured scorn on all that it signifies. Yet Christian leaders have sensed the need and the mood of our time, and responded. They are helped by the fact that a strong minority of Christians have throughout the past two millennia practiced meditation, using techniques remarkably similar to those taught by Buddhists. The leaders of this minority, such as Mother Julian and Meister Echkart, have produced some of the finest spiritual writings in the world. The huge popularity of these writings today, which far exceeds any past interest, is a measure of how rapidly Christianity is changing – how rapidly it is adopting the face of Zen. And numerous popular books re-interpret the teachings of Jesus Christ himself on lines that make him appear like a Zen master.

In contrast to western Europe, the Islamic world appears to be enjoying a resurgence of theological religion. Many mosques are fuller than ever for Friday prayers, many imams preach sermons insisting on strict adherence to traditional Islamic doctrines, and many young men are keen to study the Quran – which means also becoming familiar with the classical Arabic in which the Quran was written. And, of course, Islam is the primary breeding ground of militant religiosity, in which people are willing to use violence in order to promote their religious ideas. Although religious militancy is a complex phenomenon, a major attraction is that it offers an antidote to the humiliation felt by many Muslims at their economic, and thence also political, domination by the West. Thus if Muslim countries were to experience a sustained period of economic growth, raising them towards equality with the West, militant religiosity would fade and the cultural and educational changes wrought by prosperity would, as in Europe, undermine the theology on which militancy is based. The current resurgence of theological Islam may prove to be like the evangelical revivals within Christianity in the nineteenth century, which prompted many to think that theological Christianity was enjoying a new springtime, but which in retrospect appear like a final burst of theological sunshine before the onset of winter.

Like Christianity Islam has its own tradition of spirituality on which it can draw. In fact, in their heyday the Sufi mystics of the Middle East enjoyed far greater influence and respect than the Christian mystics ever did in Europe, and their literature is no less fine. In their appetite for guidance of self-transformation, a growing number of westerners are studying Sufism. So when the religion of self-transformation begins to impinge on Islam, Muslims will be able to feel pride at the global respect in which their own masters of spirituality are held.

In trying to fulfill their global ambitions both Christianity and Islam created global organizations. In the case of Islam religious and political institutions were from the outset closely integrated – which helps to explain why the economic and political weakness of Islamic nations has such profound religious repercussions. And the power of the mosque and the church alike was underpinned by the obligation on ordinary adherents to attend corporate worship once a week – enabling the religious hierarchy both to instill theology and to extract money. The religion of self-transformation by contrast has no need either for large organizations or for regular corporate worship – although it tends to place a high value on beautiful religious buildings, and even on occasional rituals. Thus Muslim clerics are doomed to experience the steady loss in status that most of their Christian counterparts have long been suffering, and the statistics of knees on prayer-mats will decline. But then both Jesus and Muhammad showed scant respect for the clerics of their own time.

INVESTING IN THE POOR

Only one country in history has enjoyed sustained economic growth without substantial funds from other countries: that country is Britain, who was the first to industrialize. And the rate of growth was by modern standards very slow: in the final decades of the eighteenth century and the early decades of the nineteenth, output per head probably rose by little more than one percent each year. Through the latter half of the nineteenth century British investors were funding the industrialization of the US, and the Asian tigers such as South Korea and Malaysia, whose economies often grew at more than ten percent a year in 1970s and 80s, sucked in funds from all over the world. Indeed, such was the enthusiasm of foreign investors for the Asian tigers that their economies achieved in two or three decades what took Britain two centuries. And once an economy has been set in motion, it gathers its own momentum, as its own people use their extra income to provide further funds, so the proportion of capital owned by foreigners soon starts to fall.

Despite the success of the Asian tigers, many countries in Asia, and most countries in Africa, remain imprisoned in poverty; and in some cases living standards are actually falling. Political turmoil has undoubtedly formed the prison walls: no one will invest funds in businesses whose assets may be seized or destroyed at any moment, and whose workers live in perpetual fear of attack. But, while the plight of some countries such as the Congo and Zimbabwe is worse than ever, in other countries there seem to be stable governments that are capable of protecting people and property. And the potential for investment in these countries is huge. Their low wages would give them a strong competitive edge in world markets, especially in industries that are labor intensive. Then, as workers in export industries spent their wages, there would be opportunities for local firms to produce the goods they want – which in turn would inject more demand into the economy, and hence more opportunities for business. The Asian tigers built their economies on large-scale manufacturing, since at the time it was still only possible to export tangible goods. The advent of digital technology enables newly developing economies to export services as well, such as data processing. In India there are now several call centers dealing with customers in Britain and the US. At present returns on investment in the affluent countries are sufficiently high to give little incentive to seek opportunities in the poorer countries, and after so many years of unrest, it will take more time for the political improvements in Africa to seem secure. But as savings rise in the affluent countries and returns on investments fall, so the poorer countries will steadily become more and more attractive. Transnational companies will establish an increasing proportion of their production facilities there, and private individuals will be willing to put money into local firms. In the nineteenth century great merchant banks such as Barings, which had agents in every city and town, were the main means by which funds were channeled from Britain to new enterprises in America, and they also offered advice to those enterprises about foreign markets. In the same way adventurous financial institutions in America and Europe will acquire specialist knowledge of businesses in the poor countries of Africa and Asia, then they will provide the means by which ordinary people in the affluent countries can pool their money, and invest in a range of businesses, thereby minimizing risk.

Local enterprises backed by western funds are undoubtedly preferable to transnational corporations. Transnational corporations generally have little commitment to the countries in which they base their production facilities, and are notoriously willing to shift those facilities elsewhere in the pursuit of some small financial gain. Some corporations have a shameful record of political interference for their own benefit. But local enterprises typically lack technological and managerial expertise, and they can often overcome this lack by recruiting people that have worked in transnational corporations – a practice known as technology transfer. Thus in the early stages of development a mixture of transnational and local businesses is desirable, with local businesses becoming more and more important as the economy grows.

During the past four decades governments in affluent countries, with varying degrees of generosity, have given money to the poorer countries. Some of this money has provided food and shelter in emergencies; some has helped to supply basic needs, such as clean water and efficient sewerage; and some has built roads, schools and clinics. Some too has been wasted on projects such as dams and airports that appealed to the egos of ambitious politicians, and some has disappeared into the private accounts of politicians. Yet, as in every country that has risen out of poverty in the past, the key is what Keynes called people's 'animal spirits' – their spirit of enterprise. Thus the most valuable forms of foreign aid are those that encourage this spirit. In particular, foreign aid can hasten the technology transfer by providing expert advisers and consultants to local enterprises, and by enabling talented young men and women to study in European and American universities. And, as has already happened in several countries, western experts can help set up efficient financial markets – these would initially channel western funds to local enterprises, and later would channel the savings of local people themselves.

In recent years many people in the West have become uneasy about the effect on poorer countries of western financial institutions, especially the International Monetary Fund (IMF) and the World Trade Organization (WTO), and major demonstrations of protest have been held at their meetings. The officials of the WTO have been so unnerved by these demonstrations that its new round of trade negotiations was inaugurated in the Gulf state of Qatar, from where protesters could be easily excluded. The WTO, under the name of the

General Agreement on Tariffs and Trade, was founded after the Second World War to promote free international trade, in the belief that all countries gain from it, and it now exerts great pressure on poorer countries to abolish trade restrictions. And the IMF, founded in the same period, frequently makes the liberalization of trade a condition of its loans to poorer countries. While free trade between equal partners undoubtedly brings mutual benefits, the protestors are right in claiming that free trade between highly unequal partners favors the rich at the expense of the poor. When America industrialized in the late nineteenth century, its federal government erected massive trade barriers to protect its infant enterprises from cheap imports from Britain and the rest of Europe. It lifted these barriers only when the infants had grown into strapping adults, and could compete successfully. When Japan set about rebuilding her devastated economy after her defeat in 1945, America wisely encouraged the erection of import tariffs, and more recently the Asian tigers have followed Japan's example. Arguably both America and Japan retained their tariffs for too long, allowing local firms to become complacent and inefficient, but without tariffs the people of America and Japan would still be digging the soil and drawing water from wells.

The protestors accuse the IMF and WTO of being instruments of western interests. If this accusation is justified, and if the IMF and WTO are shrewd in serving the West, then their policies will change as the savings rate in the West rises. Western households will have a direct financial interest in the success of businesses in the poorer countries, and hence will benefit from trade barriers that allow these businesses to sell their goods into local markets. The IMF and WTO can use their expertise to judge the right height of the barriers, and also the right time to lower them.

ECOLOGY ON THE CHEAP

During the nineteenth and early twentieth centuries London was famous for its thick winter fogs: the smoke from coal fires billowed from millions of chimneys, and in certain climatic conditions it was forced downwards in such thickness that Londoners compared it with pea soup. Then in the late 1940s the rulers of the city announced that in a few years time they would ban the use of coal, district by district. The suppliers of coal strongly objected. But when their protests went unheeded, they started to manufacture coke instead, and many richer households switched to central heating using gas and oil. So by the time coal was outlawed, the pea soup fogs had already ceased, people were breathing freely – and the financial cost had been minimal.

More recently in the 1980s a similar chain of events occurred when it was discovered that CFCs in aerosols and refrigerators were depleting the ozone layer in the upper atmosphere. Several governments announced that in a few years time they would forbid the use of CFCs in new products. Manufacturers of aerosols and refrigerators variously claimed that CFCs were essential, or that the development of alternatives would prove long and expensive. But governments stood firm, and cheap alternatives were quickly found so by the time the ban came into force, it was hardly needed.

These stories show the power of collective action against pollution, and they also illustrate human ingenuity and adaptability, so the costs of collective action are usually far less than is originally feared. But collective action against the most important form of pollution, the emission of 'greenhouse gases' that may cause global warming, has proved horribly elusive. After many years of negotiation the major polluting nations reached an agreement at Kyoto that promised merely to limit further increases in emissions. In 2001 the new American president, George W Bush, announced that he would not ratify the agreement, since it would damage American industry and living standards. And he expressed doubt about the link between pollution and global warming, claiming that it remains unproven.

While a degree of genuine doubt remains, the potential damage from global warming is so great that the scales of risk are weighted massively on the side of collective action. Yet the scales of politics have two equally heavy weights on the side of inaction. First, western affluence is far more dependent on oil, the main source of greenhouse gases, than it ever was on CFCs or even coal, and it uses oil in a wide variety of different ways. While technologies using alternatives to oil are already being developed, the current timescale for putting them into widespread use stretches to decades rather than years, so it is easy to imagine that any quick reductions in oil consumption would cause palpable hardship. Secondly, whereas the people of London experienced a direct and immediate link between the banning of coal and cleaner air, the present generation would enjoy no benefit from reducing greenhouse gas emissions. At best there might be fewer droughts and floods over the next few decades than there would otherwise have been, the main beneficiaries would be our grandchildren and their grandchildren, who would have a better chance of surviving and leading comfortable lives. When the horizon of democratic politics is the next election, few politicians are likely to strive for such a distant gain. So for those anxious about global warming, it is tempting to despair.

The impetus towards greater savings, combined the constraints on government spending, may, however, offer hope.

As people in the West try to reduce the time and the cost of crawling in their cars along congested roads, so they will reduce the distances they travel, and hence reduce their exhaust emissions. More importantly, just as the people of London accepted the ban on coal because they themselves enjoyed the cleaner air, so people will become more willing to accept limitations on the use of their cars because themselves will benefit. People working at home will be keen to reduce the noise and immediate pollution that cars cause. And those choosing to live closer to their places of work and amusement will mainly be making local journeys. They will stand to gain from any restrictions that enable local buses and trams to move more quickly. The most vivid example of this convergence of interests is Singapore, where the territory is so small that all journeys are local. People have cheerfully embraced severe controls on the use of cars within the city, knowing that their own lives will be made easier by leaving sufficient space for mass transit systems. Journey times are far shorter in Singapore than any city of similar size in the world – and the emission of greenhouse gases is far less.

As westerners try to save space, so they will reduce the quantity and size of the goods they possess. Instead, like the Japanese, they shall have fewer goods of higher quality and smaller size. This will reduce the number of factories in the world, and since factories around the world are major users of oil, emissions of greenhouse gases will fall still further. Moreover, smaller homes imply less money spent on heating and air-conditioning – both of which, directly or indirectly, use large amounts of oil. And in a modest way they will curtail the depletion of the planet's natural resources: small, durable goods use fewer metals and less wood than large goods that have been poorly made and must frequently be replaced.

Second only to global warming as a threat to human survival comes soil erosion. Many of the deserts of the world have been created over the past two millennia by foolish methods of agriculture and forestry. In Roman times north Africa was the granary of the empire, and the Sahara desert was confined to the center of the continent but intensive cultivation of only a narrow range of crops pulled the Sahara northwards to the Mediterranean coast. Ancient manuscripts describe the highlands of Ethiopia as a mixture of rich woodland and fertile fields, but the trees were cut down for building and firewood, so the rain washed the soil away – and also became less plentiful. Substantial chunks of Afghanistan were once irrigated by a sophisticated system of canals, but the salts from the water poisoned the soil and made it barren. These ecological catastrophes unfolded slowly, so, as with global warming today, people did not suffer the consequences of their own folly, but bequeathed them to their descendents. And sadly the follies of the past are being repeated today in many parts of Africa and Asia, and so the deserts continue to grow – in places the Sahara is spreading southwards by over a kilometer each year.

In recent decades humanity has invented a new way to destroy nature's bounty: the abundant use of agricultural chemicals. These chemicals not only damage the soil directly, but they also reduce the incentive to use natural fertilizers, especially animal manure, which both feed the soil and strengthen its structure. Dust storms in the prairies of north America and the lowlands of Europe are symptoms of this technological madness – and it can be readily confirmed by picking up a clod from a field, and comparing it with soil in a woodland or garden that has not been contaminated. It is quite conceivable that within a century or two the American prairies and the European lowlands will have turned into new Saharas.

Since organic methods of farming, which avoid agricultural chemicals, are generally more labor intensive, their products tend to be slightly more expensive. And since only a small minority consumes them, transport and handling costs tend to be higher, adding to the final price. This means that the impetus towards higher savings may in the first instance reduce demand for them. However, most religions of self-transformation teach the importance of healthy eating, so as more and more people try to save by investing in their own well being, demand for organic foods is likely to rise. This in turn will cause handling and transport costs to fall, and the price of organic foods will move closer and closer to that of foods sprayed with chemicals. Moreover, the producers of agricultural machinery will be spurred to produce new types of equipment that reduce the labor intensity of organic production, reducing price still further. It is even possible that, when the majority of people are eating organically, there will no premium to pay.

Although the pea soup fogs of London had been endemic for at least a century and half, the government only felt able to ban coal fires when alternative means of heating had become available, so the discomfort and inconvenience of a ban would be small. Similarly strong collective action on global warming and soil erosion will become possible as and when the apparent personal costs of such action fall. And once the prospect of such action looms, the race to develop alternative technologies will accelerate. So as journeys become more local, local governments will feel more confident in restricting the use of cars in favor of public transport networks. Then, as public transport networks become more widespread, central governments will feel more confident in accepting international limitations on the use of oil. This in turn will raise the potential rewards for inventing and manufacturing sources of locomotion and power that do not need oil – and human ingenuity, as it always has done in the past, will respond. In the same way, as more people decide to eat organically, governments will feel more confident about putting restrictions on the use of chemicals. This will raise the cost of non-organic food, giving a further spur to demand for organic food, and a further incentive to the invention of machines that help organic production.

If a ban on coal fires had never been imposed on London, there would have been a slow and modest improvement in the quality of the air, as people gradually shifted to other forms of heating, but even today London might still suffer from the occasional pea-souper, caused by those who remained wedded to coal. Similarly, a greater desire for saving will bring some modest improvements in humanity's relationship with its environment. However, an initial shift to other forms of heating in post-War showed that the cost of collective action to individual households would be low compared with the benefits; so a ban on coal fires became politically feasible. Similarly, the main effect of higher saving will be to reduce the cost to individuals of collective ecological action, and to increase the benefits – thereby making collective action far more likely to occur.

WORKING FOR CREDIT

Markets for goods and services exist because production and consumption are separate: one person or group produces goods or services, and sells them to another person who consumes them. Of course, in a modern economy there may be two or three intermediaries between the producer and the consumer, such as a wholesaler, a retailer, an advertising agency, and so on; but these intermediaries are really producing services that contribute to what the consumer ultimately buys. Markets for capital, which are the essence of capitalism, exist because the saving and investing of capital are separate: consumers save part of their income to spend later, and producers invest those savings in machinery, office and factory buildings, and the like – with banks, stock markets, and the various other financial institutions acting as intermediaries. This means that most people in the modern world lead a double economic life: for a certain number of hours each week they are producers, working and investing, and for the other hours of the week they are consumers, spending and saving.

Markets for goods have existed for many thousands of years, even in tribal societies. Long before Europeans arrived, Aboriginal tribes on the coast of Australia were producing tools and ornaments that found their way to tribes deep in the heart of the continent, conveyed through a series of exchanges between one tribe and another. But for most of human history only a very few special items were bought and sold, while the bulk of goods and services were produced by the group that also consumed them – people grew their own food, built their own homes, educated their own children, and nursed their own sick. The process of industrialization, which began in Britain in the late eighteenth century, depended on a huge extension of the scope of markets. Within barely a century throughout Europe and north America the great bulk of production was taken out the home, and transferred to factories. Indeed, for most individual families this transformation from a single to a double economic life occurred within a few weeks: they left their ancestral homes in the countryside where they worked for themselves and their families, and they moved to a town where they worked for wages.

Yet even in the industrial towns people clung tenaciously to the notion that families should retain direct involvement in education and health care. Many of the original urban schools were co-operative enterprises, run by families within a neighborhood for the benefit of their own children. Even when a rich philanthropist or some charitable organization owned and ran a school, the children's families were often closely involved, maintaining and cleaning the buildings, organizing sports, and even buying books. When anyone in a family fell sick, the other members of the family, helped by neighbors, looked after them at home. And there were networks of local people, usually elderly women, respected for their knowledge of medical remedies, who would prescribe treatment. Only in extreme cases did a family call a doctor – who had to be paid.

These local arrangements for education and health care varied greatly in quality. And they were generally regarded as inferior to the arrangements that the wealthy elite were now making, in which they purchased almost every aspect of education and health care. Indeed, the upper classes in Britain typically sent their boys away at the age of seven to remote boarding schools, where they stayed for ten months of the year. So when in the mid twentieth century western governments took responsibility for the provision of education and health care to the whole population, their declared intention was to raise the standards of the majority close to that of the minority. And inevitably they imposed a strict separation of production from consumption: those working in the educational and medical services funded by the state are quite distinct from those consuming the services.

Although no one can doubt the improvements in education and health care over the past half-century, the separation of production and consumption in these spheres has a heavy cost. Teachers frequently complain of the lack of parental commitment to the education of their children, and problems of indiscipline and low attainment are attributed to the indifference of parents. Yet, since parents have no influence on their children's education, and no role in the schools their children attend, their commitment cannot be nurtured. Doctors and nurses know that the love of relatives and friends is an essential element in the healing process. Yet, by reducing the role of relatives and friends in determining and delivering the treatment of illness, the state has reduced the scope for this love to be expressed.

The perpetual and worsening crisis in public services to which western societies are now condemned, along with a rise in the impetus to save, offers the possibility of combining the old approach to education and health care with modern improvements. Instead of being funded from taxation, educational and medical services would revert to charging fees for their services and the tax rate would be reduced accordingly. Then people would be invited to offer their time to their schools, colleges, hospitals and clinics in their locality and they would be encouraged to acquire additional skills that were required. In return for their time and skill they would earn some form of credit that they could use in the future – for the education of their children and grandchildren, and for their own medical treatment. The number of these credit workers, and the skills that they could offer, would determine the extent to which they replaced those being paid a salary – probably salary workers would continue to perform the most highly skilled jobs, while credit workers took over many lesser tasks.

Credit working would formalize the kind of relationship that many people had with local schools in the nineteenth and early twentieth centuries, and it would have at least four important benefits. First, it would be a means of saving that would not be subject to the vagaries of the financial markets. Second, many would find working for a few hours each week for a school or hospital very satisfying. By the time they reach middle-age people are often becoming quite bored with their normal job, so they would welcome the opportunity to reduce the number of hours they worked at it, and to become part of a community whose purpose was the care of others. Indeed, their credit work might re-invigorate their normal work. Third, elderly people could continue and even extend their credit working beyond the age when they had retired from their normal job. Many of the tasks in education and health care require sensitivity and patience – qualities that grow with age. Thus credit work would both take advantage of our longer life expectancy, and reduce the proportion of the population that is economically dependent. Fourth, people would tend to work at the hospitals and clinics where they themselves would be treated, and the schools and colleges where their own children and grandchildren were educated. Thus to some degree the link between production and consumption would be restored.

When in the twentieth century western governments became directly involved in the provision of education and health care, their methods of involvement took two forms. In some countries, such as Britain, the state simply took over most of the existing schools and hospitals, and thus became the direct employer of their staff. In other countries the state allowed existing institutions to remain independent, and it became a kind of banker and insurer, requiring people to pay monthly contributions, and then financing medical and educational needs as they arose. In most countries there is a somewhat awkward and haphazard mixture of both methods. The introduction of credit working would clearly require that educational and health care institutions be independent of the state. However, the state could, and perhaps should, continue to function as banker and insurer – the difference being that people could make part or all of their monthly contributions in the form of credit work. Thus the credit earned by people through credit work could be given a money value, equivalent to the wage that would be paid for the work, and educational and health care institutions would pay that sum on behalf of each credit worker to the state insurance bank. Then, as and when people needed medical treatment, the state insurance bank would pay the fees, and people would also be entitled to a certain level of fees for the education of their direct descendents.

Western governments have also used education and health care as channels through which the poor benefit at the expense of the rich. The taxation or compulsory insurance levied on people is generally proportionate to their income, or even progressive, rising more than proportionately with income. Thus the rich pay far more than the poor for the same educational and health care services. The introduction of credit work would make this impossible, since people's credits could only be valued according to the value of their work. Thus payments to the state insurance bank, in the form of both credit work and money, would have to function like any normal insurance payments: the rich and poor alike would pay the same for the same eventual benefits.

This system would be more honest and it would remove the economic disincentive effects of proportionate and progressive taxes. It would also allow private insurance companies to compete with the state, ensuring that the state insurance bank remained efficient, and allowing people to pay additional premiums for additional benefits. The only element of compulsion is that everyone would be required to take out basic health insurance, and everyone with children would have to take out basic educational insurance, or grandparents would do so on their behalf – just as at present everyone with a car has to take out basic driving insurance. Unemployed people without major disabilities would be required to perform a certain amount of credit work but those unable to work, and those on low incomes, could apply to have some or all of their insurance contributions paid by the government out of tax revenues. In most western countries the net effect on government finances would be to cut taxation by around a quarter – and, of course, the remaining taxes would remain proportionate or progressive.

POPULATION BALANCE

In Britain in the late nineteenth century the incomes of ordinary workers, which had hitherto been near to subsistence levels, began to rise significantly and as this occurred, the birth rate of working families began to fall. This was the first appearance of a phenomenon that has been replicated in every continent and culture: rising incomes are almost always and everywhere associated with declining birth rates. The speed of decline varies somewhat from place to place. In Italy and Germany it is now around 1.4 children per woman, while in Britain it is nearer 2 – all places of roughly similar income per family. Figures in the Asian tiger economies vary from around 1.7 in South Korea and Singapore, to 3.4 in Malaysia and the Philippines. But despite local differences, the overall pattern is the same.

This negative link between birth rates and incomes contradicts most previous ideas about population change. In

1798 the economist Thomas Malthus pronounced that the population tends to double or triple with every generation, and is only checked by limits on the food available to feed hungry mouths. And soon afterwards David Ricardo spoke of an iron law of wages: that whenever wages rise above subsistence, the population will rise and the additional number of workers will bring wages down again. Thus according to Malthus and Ricardo the link between birth rates and incomes is positive: as people's incomes rise, they will have more children. This view became widespread; and in the 1830s help given to the poor in Britain was drastically reduced, on the grounds that they would merely produce more children, thereby worsening their poverty (+). And even as late as the 1970s many people were convinced that the global population was destined to continue growing indefinitely, until the earth's ability to produce food was utterly exhausted.

The negative link also appears stronger than all moral and social forces opposing it. The Roman Catholic Church has persistently opposed artificial methods of limiting fertility, and has tended to encourage large families. Yet Italy, whose population is predominantly Catholic, has experienced one of the steepest declines in fertility in the world. During the 1960s and 70s the Indian government made strenuous efforts to promote birth control, with posters in every village extolling small families, free contraceptives, and even at one time free vasectomies. The birth rate, however, remained stubbornly high – until in the 1980s incomes began to rise.

It is possible that better education is a factor. As people become richer, their children tend to spend more years at school. So when the children become adults, they are better informed about how to control their fertility, and they may also be more willing to ignore any religious teaching or cultural prejudice against artificial contraception. But this assumes that human beings naturally want small families, and will therefore keep their families small as soon as they know how. It seems more likely that poorer people actually want bigger families and that richer people want smaller ones. Thus human beings make an economic choice about how many children to have, weighing the benefits and costs, and at different levels of income the relative benefits and costs change.

The main economic benefit to poorer couples of having children is that their children are their pension: when they grow old, their children will care and provide for them, just as they care and provide for their own parents. Moreover, poor families often live in conditions where disease is rife, and they have little access to medical treatment, so their children have a significant chance of dying before they reach adulthood. Hence to ensure that some of their children survive, couples must have many children. By comparison the costs of additional children are quite small. An extra child is an extra mouth to feed, but at a quite a young age children start working, and thereby contribute to the domestic economy. And since most mothers in poor communities work at home, they can readily combine their work with the raising of children.

As people become richer, the chances of their children surviving into adulthood rise and they are also able to put aside money for their old age. So the economic benefits of having a large family fall. But the costs rise. A larger house is needed, and housing is disproportionately expensive in rich communities. Probably also a larger car is required, plus all the other goods and services that richer children expect. Most children remain in education until their late teens or early twenties, and then leave the parental home, so they make little or no contribution at any stage to the domestic economy. And in modern capitalist economies, where most women are in full-time gainful work, a further, even greater cost arises: the cost of time. Parents must choose between working fewer hours in order to raise their children, or paying others to help raise their children – and either option is expensive.

There is, however, a cruel paradox in the negative link between birth rates and incomes. While for a poor couple it is wise and rational to have a large family, for a poor country large families are profoundly damaging. Any economic growth in the country can be completely absorbed by the increasing population. Thus in the past three decades, although the countries of sub-Saharan Africa have achieved some modest growth, incomes per head have fallen sharply because the birth rate has been so high. And rising population puts pressure on the environment, making further growth even more difficult. The main reason for the spread of the Sahara Desert is that families are forced to collect firewood from its southern fringe, and as they destroy the sparse trees and shrubs, the barren sands take over. The pressure to grow food on fragile, marginal land hastens the erosion of topsoil. Thus while poor countries have high birth rates, the high birth rates tend to keep them poor – so they are locked in a vicious circle of poverty and fertility.

Higher saving in the affluent West, inducing westerners to invest in the poor countries of the world, offers the prospect of breaking this circle. New factories and plants, employing large numbers of people, can begin to pull wages above subsistence level. Then, as in Britain in the late nineteenth century, the birth rate will start to fall. This means that further economic growth actually raises living standards, causing the birth rate to fall further. Hence the vicious circle becomes a virtuous one. It takes two or three decades, however, for a falling birth rate affect significantly the total population – a phenomenon known as 'population momentum'. This is because there remain large numbers of young women at the age of motherhood, who were products of the earlier high birth rate. Only when the products of a lower birth rate reach the age of maternity does the population trend begin to shift. Thus to break the vicious circle affluent westerners must sustain their investment in the poor over a long period. And this means that political stability in poor countries, which is the essential condition for attracting investment, must also be sustained.

The AIDS epidemic, however, poses a severe threat to any prospect of breaking the circle. By raising the chance of people dying in childhood and early adulthood, it encourages parents to have more children in the hope that some will survive. Worse still, the rate of infection is highest amongst skilled males in cities: they are often cut off from their families, they have money, and easy access to casual sex, and their macho culture often involves a denial of the dangers. Their loss is a severe blow to existing businesses, and makes it more difficult for new businesses to start. However, in countries like Senegal and Uganda, whose governments have organized coherent campaigns to increase awareness and to distribute condoms, infection rates are falling quite steeply. The cost of such campaigns is relatively small by western standards, so providing finance for them would be a form of foreign aid with an extremely high return.

Meanwhile in western countries the death rate has fallen so low that it may soon stimulate an increase in the birth rate. As we have seen, longer life expectancy will induce high savings, which in turn will reduce the returns on savings. Thus many people may find themselves quite poor in their final years. Their offspring, who at that stage are at the height of their earning power, may then feel impelled to offer help. Thus the material bond that the West has largely broken, between middle-aged people and their ageing parents, may be restored; children will once more become an economic benefit, and not just a cost. Couples without children, who are now envied for the luxuries they can afford, will again be pitied for lacking any prospect of family support in their later years, and families with two or three children will again be admired. This shift in attitudes may happen quite soon. Over the next decade the baby-boomers born after the Second World War will be retiring and many will be shocked at the smallness of the pension that their accumulated savings will buy. Those with middle-aged offspring to subsidize their pension will look back at the cost of child rearing as an excellent investment.

No one knows how many billions of human beings, all enjoying some degree of prosperity, the planet can support. Ever since Malthus offered his grim warning, people have tended to imagine that the global population of their own time has marked the upper limit. Yet the population has continued to rise, and the production of food has risen by approximately the same amount. Nonetheless both the natural environment and the global economy would probably benefit from a steady decline in total numbers. Higher savings in the affluent West is the most powerful, and perhaps the only, means of moving towards this. As returns on savings in the West fall, so the birth rate in the West will rise. And as westerners seek higher returns on their savings by investing in poor countries, so the birth rate in poor countries will fall. Looking at the present pattern of birth rates, it seems quite conceivable that the long-term birth rate of a prosperous world with long life expectancy is around two children per female – a little below the replacement rate.

PART 4: ECONOMICAL SAVING

THE INVISIBLE HAND

In 1776 Adam Smith, the great apostle of capitalism and the founder of economics as a coherent discipline, wrote of an invisible hand that uses the selfish actions of individuals to attain prosperity for society as a whole. A worker takes the job that gives the highest wage and, since employers pay wages according to the value of what workers produce, the best-paid job is also the most productive. An investor puts money into a business that yields the highest profit and, since profits reflect the value of what businesses sell, the most profitable business also satisfies its customers best. Households spend their income according to their own needs and wants and, since businesses must respond to their customers' demands, this ensures that the whole economy is operating in the best interests of the people within it.

   Adam Smith did not believe that human beings are incorrigibly selfish, he recognized that they often act unselfishly towards their relatives and friends. But in economic matters he believed that self-interest generally rules. And his analysis of capitalism led him to the conclusion that, within the economic sphere, truth and goodness happily coincide: people's actual behavior, selfish as it is, conforms to how they ought to behave.

If my analysis within this book is correct, the invisible hand will soon be at work in relation to people's savings. There are at least five reasons why self-interested, rational people in the affluent West will start to become thriftier. And, since people in economic matters tend to act in a self-interested manner, we can predict that the overall rate of saving in the West will rise. This will have at least five consequences that are desirable for humanity as a whole – in relation to religion, the poor countries of the world, the natural environment, the provision of education and health care, and population.

At the heart of Adam Smith's analysis is a further insight: that the small and even trivial decisions of individuals can have huge power. Individuals decide to wear trainers instead of shoes – as a result the entire footwear industry is transformed. Individuals decide that it is more convenient to travel by car rather than bus or train –as a result a revolution occurs in the transport system. And this insight has guided the present book. The decision by individual households over how much to spend and save seems quite small and unimportant. Yet, as Marx and Keynes understood, on this decision hangs the entire future of our economic system. Stubbornly high rates of saving are currently shaking the Japanese economy, and as Japanese thrift spreads to the West, so there will be a global economic earthquake.

Adam Smith was not only a shrewd observer of economic events, he wanted to influence events. By showing how capitalism works, he wanted to encourage people into becoming better capitalists, and to encourage governments into lifting restrictions on the development of capitalism. By the 1790s British politicians such as William Pitt were using Smith's arguments to advocate the abolition of trade tariffs. And in the early nineteenth century progressive parents employed teachers familiar with Smith's writings to show their children the virtues of capitalist enterprise. Smith has often been accused of painting too sunny a picture of capitalism, as if the invisible hand were divine. But he was committed to capitalism, and while he acknowledged some of its problems and flaws, he was eager to persuade people of its benefits.

In this book I have not only suggested that the rate of savings is likely to increase in the West, but I have also urged it to happen. If you would describe yourself as an affluent westerner, then it is an appeal to you to save a little more and spend a little less of your income – or even merely to save more and spend less of all additional income. The appeal is primarily to your self-interest: saving more and spending less is in the present circumstances a wise, rational and shrewd thing to do. And it is also an appeal to conscience: the world as a whole will be greatly helped by a higher rate of saving in the West.

This begs the question of what form this extra savings should take. Broadly speaking you can save in two ways: you can invest in material assets, and you can invest in yourself. So what are likely to be the best material assets? And what is the most effective way of investing in oneself?

ACQUIRING MATERIAL ASSETS

There are two main types of material assets. The first is real estate, such as houses, office buildings, and agricultural land, and the income takes the form of rents. The second is financial assets, such as shares, bonds, and cash, and the income takes the form of dividends and interest. In choosing between different assets investors must take into account not only the likely income, but also the potential for capital appreciation – for the asset itself to grow in value. In this regard there is an important difference between bonds and cash. With a bond, such as a government bond and a company debenture, the income is fixed, but, since bonds are sold on stock markets, the capital value varies. In general, if interest rates rise, the capital value of existing bonds falls, and vice versa. With cash, in the form of an interest-bearing account at a bank or similar institution, the capital value is fixed, but the income varies according to the prevailing rate of interest, which is determined by the central bank.

The example of Japan suggests that, when savings are high, the value of most material assets fall. Anyone investing in real estate ten or twelve years ago would have lost over half their wealth, and anyone investing in shares would have seen their wealth shrink to only a quarter of its former size. Wise investors with a gift of foresight would initially have put their money into a bank, but since interest rates have fallen so low, and some banks seem to be wobbling, it might now be wiser to take the money out, and stuff it in a mattress. However, high savings have not in themselves been responsible for this decline in values. Low spending by consumers, combined with a degree of corruption and laxity amongst business leaders, has squeezed the profit margins of many Japanese businesses, and hence reduced dividends. Japanese households have reacted by investing abroad, especially in America, buying share and bonds in dollars. Indeed this outflow of funds has enabled America to import far more goods than it exports, without causing a collapse of the dollar. The Japanese are in effect lending America the money to maintain its profligate life style. As a result the demand for Japanese shares and real estate has fallen, and so prices have plummeted.

But if savings were to rise in all the affluent countries of the world, the reaction would be rather different. Although lack of consumption would squeeze companies' profit margins and dividends, households would still buy their shares, because they could not readily buy shares elsewhere. Thus while dividends fell slightly, share prices would rise, so the returns on shares would drop. Similarly, as households direct their savings towards bonds, bond prices would rise, and since the interest payments are constant, the returns on bonds – interest payments as a percentage of their price – would fall. And if they tried to buy property as an investment, property prices would rise while rents remained stable or even fell, so the returns on property would also fall.

There would, however, be substantial variations between different types of share and property. Insofar as people save by buying durable goods of high quality, then companies producing such goods will have healthy profits and will expand, so their dividends will steadily rise. When the savings rate starts to rise, you would be wise to invest in these companies. Insofar as people try to reduce their expenditure by saving space, they will tend to move to smaller houses and apartments that are well designed, and insofar as they want to save the time they spend on congested roads, they will want such houses and apartments near to town and city centers, or near to good public transport routes. So if you wish to invest in property, buy houses and apartments that fit this description, as their prices are likely to rise fastest and furthest.

As and when financial institutions such as investment banks find efficient ways of channeling funds to poorer countries, then you should take advantage of those channels. The sooner you invest in companies in poorer countries, the larger your eventual returns will be. But there will inevitably be significant political and economic risks attached to these countries and companies. So you should spread your investments quite widely between different countries and companies. It is probable that investment banks will have a range of funds into which you can put money, each fund specializing in a different market, hence spreading your money should be quite straightforward.

As Marx and Keynes both convincingly showed, it is almost impossible to exaggerate the enormity of the consequences of higher savings. And even if my analysis of these consequences, as they might unfold in the modern world, is broadly correct, it is bound to contain mistakes and misjudgments. Moreover, there are bound to be variations between one affluent country and another, which could distort the prices of asset values. Thus, for example, if the rate of savings rises much faster and higher in Germany than in France, French property prices in cities may remain stagnant while urban property prices in Germany may shoot up. In the light of this high degree of uncertainty you should retain some of your savings as cash, in the form of an account at a bank that bears interest. It is possible that western economies will react to higher savings differently from the Japanese economy, with prices falling quite steeply, in accordance with Ricardo's theory. If this occurs, cash will appreciate in value, since falling prices – 'negative inflation', as it is sometimes known – implies that the value of money is rising. And if you do not like banks, you could keep a stash of notes and coins at home, but use a locked safe rather than a mattress, and remember to raise your home insurance premium!

ACQUIRING PERSONAL ASSETS

When economists describe people's motivation, they use a term adopted from the philosopher Jeremy Bentham: they say that people are trying to maximize their 'utility'. In Bentham's usage utility means pleasure minus pain, and human happiness is simply total pleasure minus total pain. Thus economists are really saying that human beings try to be happy. But Bentham went even further than this, and for practical purposes most economists have been inclined to follow him. He asserted that human happiness is directly related to income: that as people have more money to spend, they become happier. While he recognized that an additional dollop of money brings less extra happiness to a rich person than a poor person, nonetheless happiness continues to rise with wealth.

In placing happiness as life's goal, Bentham was following a hallowed western tradition going back to ancient Greece. Aristotle used the term *eudaimonia* to describe the supreme human good, and it is usually translated as happiness or fulfillment. But for Aristotle the route to happiness lay mainly in the acquisition of virtue. He distinguished two kinds of virtues: mental virtues that lead to intellectual wisdom, and moral virtues that lead to practical wisdom. Another important Greek philosopher, Epicurus, who also made happiness the goal of life, regarded happiness as consisting of freedom from all anxiety. He proposed that people should learn to take pleasure in simplicity, acquiring a taste for foods like barley cake and drinking only water, because dependence on luxuries engenders anxiety about becoming poor. The Stoic philosophers believed that happiness consisted in learning to live according to nature.

In most of the centuries that divide the ancient Greeks from Bentham, Christianity dominated western thought. Jesus himself often spoke of happiness, teaching that love is the means to it – even if love demands material sacrifices. Unlike most of the Greek philosophers, Jesus believed that human love and its joys survive death. Many of his later followers, however, emphasized the joys of love after death at the expense of those during life. And they developed a scheme of salvation that could involve great mental and physical suffering on earth in order to attain heavenly rewards. The ideas propounded by Bentham, who was an atheist, were to some degree a reaction against this scheme.

Most people in the West today, even if they remain devoted to Jesus' teachings, reject the traditional scheme of salvation. And, as we have explored in this book, people are also turning away from Bentham's crude equation of happiness with income. But they are not generally turning to Aristotle and Epicurus for guidance. Instead they are looking eastwards to some of the teachings of Hinduism, Taoism and Buddhism – including Zen. And here you find two distinct and complementary types of discipline.

The first type of discipline is psychological, involving some kind of meditation. The yoga meditation of India, which is similar to the meditation taught by the Buddha, involves concentrating the mind, and thereby attaining a state of consciousness that is different from both waking and dreaming. In this state of consciousness the mind is both quite alert, and also suggestible; so it is a state in which mental and emotional habits can gradually be altered. Many of the psychological therapies developed in the West in the past century and a half, such as hypnotherapy, seek also to induce this state, in order to create changes in attitudes and responses. The Zen meditation of Japan, especially that taught by the Rinzai and Soto schools, involves breaking down the normal patterns of logical thought until the mind suddenly shifts to an entirely intuitive mode of functioning. The Zen approach is mirrored to some degree in those western therapies, such as therapies based on gestalt psychology, that are concerned with the way in which the mind organizes experiences and perceptions.

The second type of discipline is physical. The most famous physical disciplines are the yoga postures of India, and the ta'i chi movements of China. Both these disciplines bring direct physical benefits: yoga can, for example, be very helpful in preventing and curing problems in the spine, and t'ai chi is sometimes recommended to elderly people to improve their balance, and thereby reduce the chance of falling. They also have psychological effects, enhancing the value of meditation. Thus the most effective program for transforming the self should have both a psychological and a physical component.

In past centuries a person wanting to learn one of these psychological and physical disciplines sought out a teacher, and a good teacher might attract hundreds of pupils. In the late nineteenth and early twentieth centuries various pioneering westerners went to Asia to learn them, and some Asian teachers came to the West. Now in every city and town of Europe and north America there are courses in yoga and t'ai chi. However, the techniques can also be learnt through books and videos and for some people, who want to learn at their own pace and in their own way, these methods are preferable. Indeed, teaching yourself with the help of an illustrated book may be more similar to the ancient form of learning than attending a course. The great teachers of Asia generally conveyed their wisdom to one pupil at a time, adapting their style to each pupil's needs and inclinations.

To undertake any of these disciplines requires a substantial investment in time. And time is the basic scarce resource: all your economic choices are ultimately about how you allocate your time. When you apply for a job, you are choosing how you wish to spend the most energetic of your waking hours. When you decide how much money to spend and save, you are choosing how to use the income from your time at work – you are allocating your time between present enjoyment and future enjoyment. Deciding to undertake a personal discipline involves the most fundamental choice: the choice between influencing and improving yourself, and influencing and improving your circumstances. When you go out to work, you are using your time in order to make your circumstances happier than they would otherwise be. When you undertake a personal discipline, you are using your time to make yourself happier in any circumstances that you would otherwise be.

This book carries several messages of hope, which are linked by the theme of saving and investing. Its single most important message is that in the western world most of us have reached a point of prosperity where the investment with the highest rate of return is investing in the self.

Also by Robert Van de Weyer

The Wandering Sage

ISBN 1 903816 65 3

A gift book that distills the oral wisdom of our race in today's words.

In every human society and culture there is a fund of stories - parables, fables, legends - which encapsulate moral and spiritual values and pass those values on from one generation to the next. One of the characters found in every spiritual tradition is the wandering sage. Sometimes he has a name, such as Mulla Nasrudin or Guru Nudel. More often he is nameless. He belongs to no religious hierarchy, and has no religious affiliation.

In parts of the world this storytelling tradition still survives, and in four spiritual traditions it is especially prominent; Taoism, Sufism, the Celtic and Hasidic traditions. This collection of over 70 stories captures the flavour of timeless wisdom and counter-cultural wit that is part of our Heritage. The stories are suitable for all ages, easy to remember, and once remembered never forgotten.

Price: £4.99
Available May 2004

The Anglican Quilt

ISBN: 1 903816 89 0

Resolving the Anglican crisis over homosexuality

Foreword by Most Rev Dr Josiah Idowu-Fearon, Achbishop of Kaduna, Nigeria, and member of the Eames Commission.

This book offers a detailed plan for resolving the present crisis over homosexuality in the Anglican Church, prompted by the appointment of openly gay bishops in USA and England, and the blessing of a gay partnership in Canada. Robert Van de Weyer offers proposals both for world-wide Anglicanism and for the Church of England. Tracing the roots of the crisis back to the foundations of Anglicanism over four centuries ago, he shows why ancient divisions have grown wider in recent decades. He argues that the two sides now need separate episcopal arrangements - yet both sides have much to gain by remaining together in a single body.

Price: 9.99
Available August 2004